Developing Prosocial Communities Across Cultures

Forrest B. Tyler

Developing Prosocial Communities Across Cultures

Springer

Forrest B. Tyler
Dept. Psychology
University of Maryland, College Park, MD,
USA
College Park 20742-4411
Email, personal: ftyler@psyc.umd.edu

ISBN-13: 978-0-387-71484-4 e-ISBN-13: 978-0-387-71485-1

Library of Congress Control Number: 2007927756

Printed on acid-free paper.

9 8 7 6 5 4 3 2 1

springer.com

Contents

Preface

Over the course of a long and varied career I have engaged in many kinds of scholarly and social activities and written about them for a variety of audiences. As I finished each project, I felt both a sense of accomplishment and a sense that I had not completely answered the questions with which I was concerned. Several years ago I wrote a comprehensive book in which I sought to interrelate individual and social aspects of human conduct. It answered many questions for me but still left me unsatisfied. What was left was the hardest task we face in our lives; namely, translating our ideas, or theories as we call them in academia, into some directives for applying them so that they can make a difference in our own and other people's lives. What I have tried to do here is focus on communities as the vital link in my theories about the process between people and their environments.

In fact, it is that translation task that has been the central challenge in my life personally as well as professionally. I grew up in poverty in a small rural town during the economic depression of the 1930s in the United States. I came of age in the U. S. infantry in World War II. During that time I was taught by the adults around me that the answer to my questions and the world's injustices lay in believing what I was told and overcoming my own shortcomings. In college, as I turned to psychology for better guidance, I was told that the answer was to learn the theories I was being taught. I was faced with the unspoken assumption that applying my theoretical knowledge would solve everything, including my shortcomings.

During all of that time I was interacting with people who were members of different kinds of communities and societies. We were all trying to formulate meaningful conceptions of our selves, our lives, our experiences, and our social contexts. We were shaping and being shaped by our interactions and other social and ecological forces in our lives. But I did not know that then, so as I chose to become a clinical psychologist I continued to believe that the road to improving my own life and those of others individually and socially lay in developing and applying theories of individual change.

Instead, what I began to discover was a history of incomplete successes and failures in my own personal and professional experiences and in the world around me. I found that in most psychology and related projects, the change agents involved remained detached from the situation, seeking only to solve the problems they had isolated. They often did not evaluate their work or follow through to be sure that projects were continued. For example, community programs were developed without a clear formulation of what the developers were trying to accomplish or how their approaches and results might be relevant to the people (or groups) involved or the conditions of their lives.

I gradually became increasingly dissatisfied with this status quo and began to think that I needed to understand the specific characteristics of people, their contexts, and how the two interact. That was the only way I was going to be able to apply any of my psychological or personal knowledge to helping myself or others improve my/their lives or situations. Further, I began to realize that there is and cannot be any theoretically prescribed way to apply theoretical knowledge to solve human problems. What we have to do is learn how to become engaged with people and then to work together to understand their lives and situations and how to improve them.

Otherwise stated, people's problems are basically humanitarian, not psychological. What I have been trying to learn is how to base our psychological understandings on that humanitarian perspective. It is the most difficult challenge I have ever faced. This book is an account of my struggle and that of many others who have joined with me in facing that challenge.

In this book, I have tried to show why a prosocial community focus is essential to the accomplishment of the goals of community psychology and related fields and to describe how to create such communities. The book incorporates a multicultural, multiethnic approach with documentary research and programmatic support for its efficacy. It identifies and demonstrates the nature of the links between community and individual functioning in ways that aid readers in understanding them. It also provides examples to enable people seeking community changes to know how to effectively translate these ideas into practice.

Our communities are the basic vital social units that provide the contexts in which we learn to live together to our mutual benefit. I have focused on them here as being crucial to providing a richer and more fulfilling framework than we currently have for understanding and improving the quality of our individual and collective lives. It is my hope that readers will find this material useful as a guide for building their own prosocial communities and enriching the quality of their personal and professional lives and of those with whom they interact. This book is to use, not just to provide an intellectual exercise.

I begin the book by defining what a prosocial community is, identify its elements and relevant interrelationships, and then provide the available evidence in support of those conclusions. I have used my conceptual frameworks for encompassing and integrating these psychological and social considerations to account for how people can form prosocial communities, function within them, and change them when desired. For example, before you can begin to construct prosocial communities, you need to understand the specific characteristics of the people involved, their situations, and how the two interact. The same is true of the groups in those communities. The book establishes that only when those factors are integrated does it becomes possible to accomplish the long range task of forming prosocial communities.

In this book I think I have expressed as best I can my answer to my question about how to use our capabilities and our knowledge to improve on the quality of our individual and collective lives. The answer is that we live together as well as apart and have to engage ourselves together or we will, perhaps, destroy ourselves individually and together. I am deeply indebted to those who have enriched my life and helped me arrive at this point. Whatever errors and shortcomings are found in this text are a product of my limitations, not those of others. I hope that any such errors do not detract from the larger message I have tried to convey and that you, my readers, will find helpful ideas and suggestions as you work to build prosocial lives and communities.

Acknowledgments

It simply is not possible to acknowledge everyone who has contributed to the contents of this book and to my writing. What I will do is thank those who have been singularly important influences. First and foremost is Sandy, my wife, colleague, editor, and life companion. We have traveled to remote destinations and worked together in often confusing and uncomfortable circumstances for substantial periods of time. In doing so, we have shared some fascinating and enriching experiences. Most often we have worked hard and been richly rewarded for our efforts by the courtesy, support, and very human caring from the people we came to know. We have also spent interminable hours together trying to make sense of our experiences. Those efforts have made this book far richer in ideas than it otherwise would have been. I am more deeply indebted to her than I will ever be able to repay.

Curt Rhodes and his contribution to my understanding of prosocial issues are in evidence, particularly in Chapter Seven, which we wrote in collaboration. It provides a culmination to this book by illustrating how a prosocial community approach can be used to guide the development of what is now a nation-wide effort at providing a better quality of life for the people of Jordan, particularly their marginalized youth and families. It also provides abundant evidence of Curt's brilliance and resourcefulness as a developer of such programs. I appreciate having had the opportunity to meet, work with, and become a friend of Curt's. To learn more about his broader record and accomplishments, please turn to the biographic statement just following chapter.

Wade Pickren, a wise and thoughtful psychologist and friend, has read this manuscript in detail and contributed many important insights that have sharpened my thinking and greatly improved the message here. His gently humane and thoughtful questions have been invaluable. I am also particularly grateful to two exceptional undergraduate psychology students, Rhea Pechter and Laura Schofield. Over the course of several semesters, they have read this manuscript many times and contributed much to making it intelligible, coherent, and much more interesting to read than it would have been otherwise.

My most important source of institutional support has been the Department of Psychology at the University of Maryland, where I have spent over thirty five years. My colleagues have accommodated my often atypical activities and departures to other lands for extended periods and provided me with the office and facilitates that have enabled me to write this and earlier books. A number of universities, medical schools, clinics, community centers, and mental hospitals in the United States and in other countries have welcomed me graciously. Colleagues in all of these places have been enormously helpful in explaining how they see my world and supportive of my efforts to understand their worlds as we struggled together to understand each other. Included in that list are colleagues from the Universities of Allahabad, India; Waikato University in Hamilton, New Zealand; and Beijing University in China. In Colombia, there were the Universities of Javeriana, Los Andes, and the National University in Bogota; the Universidad del Valle, in Cali; and the Universidad del Norte, in Barranquilla. Finally, in Santiago, Chile, there was the Universidad Catolica. In addition, the National Institute of Mental Health, National Science Foundation, Agency on Aging, Office of Substance Abuse Research, the Fulbright Commission, and the Indio-American Fellowship Program as well as the University of Maryland have provided institutional and financial support without which most of my journeys and much of my work would not have been possible.

Equally vital to my understanding have been the people in many walks of life in my own and other countries with whom I have had an opportunity to know and interact. Their vitality and commitment to the joy of living (though for some under the harshest of circumstances) never cease to amaze me or rejuvenate my own spirits. Their generosity and trust in sharing their lives and experiences with me have been truly remarkable and greatly appreciated. They have given me far more in the way of insights and wisdom than I could have imagined or discovered on my own.

My editors at Springer has been supportive and understanding as I have completed this book. I am grateful to them. I hope that the response of readers will confirm for them that their investment in my book has been worthwhile.

1
Definitions and Background Issues

1.1. Background

In 1987 I was in residence for a month at the Universidad del Norte in Barranquilla while I was in Colombia on a Fulbright award and focusing on community development. I learned from them about a fascinating community development program in which their psychology department was participating. The industries in Barranquilla's harbor district, who were plagued with labor difficulties and theft, came to the University for help and offered to support and subsidize attempts to help stabilize that situation. The department formed a cooperative partnership with the industries and the surrounding, poverty stricken community where their employees lived. The partnership focused first on establishing a day care program. The university students involved the mothers in working to upgrade one of their homes each semester for use as the day care center so that she and the other mothers could attend child care classes while their children were in day care. The university and the parents of students in child development who were participating in the program feared for the students' safety. The community leaders met with the gangs in that barrio and enlisted them in protecting the students while they were in the community. The community built on these initiatives as its residents and leaders learned how to work together and push for other benefits for their community and their schools. The university participated with the community in cleaning its streets and getting the city to make other improvements. Labor stability grew and crime decreased. The program proved so attractive that nearby barrios asked to become part of it, and the program continued to spread throughout several other nearby, poor neighborhoods.

I call such communities prosocial. Much of my life's work has been directed at discovering what such communities that function together to provide for the well-being of their members are like and how to create and sustain them. The central thesis of this book is that these kinds of communities are essential to the survival and well-being of individuals and the societies in which they live. Although prosocial communities will not solve all of the world's problems nor those of individuals, they will go a long way to help correct many of the problems we and the world's communities are facing today. Further, prosocial communities that value and support a benign and nurturing quality of life for their members are essential to the alleviation and resolution of psychosocial problems.

My concerns and experiences with similar programs have led me to focus my projects, my research, and my writing on prosocial communities. The path to my present views has never been a straight line, and I don't precisely know which specific events have led me to them. However, I can describe two more of the vignettes that have provided insights for me and have led me on this journey.

In 1982, even earlier than my sojourn in Barranquilla, I was a Fulbright lecturer teaching and learning about community development at several universities in Colombia, South America. My wife and colleague had left her position as a nursing professor to accompany me. While we were there, she volunteered with a non-profit organization that worked with street youth, providing basic health care to them. The director of that group suggested that we could help even more by documenting how the street youth viewed their lives and their world. We agreed to try. As we explored the literature, we found to our surprise that, while numerous experts from several disciplines had written about the character and world view of such youth, no one had ever asked the youth for their perspective. The experts' viewpoints reflected only their own, discipline-limited outlooks about the nature and capabilities of these children. We took on the challenge of learning from the youth and found that they survived by their own resilience and by banding together in groups to find food and shelter. They were harassed and exploited by the adults around them including the police, other authorities, and even people offering to help them. However, many of the children had healthy personal characteristics, prosocial ambitions, and formed constructive relationships with other children. Unfortunately, they also felt that part of their struggle was against society's stereotypes of them. We fed that information back to people and agencies working with the youth in constructive ways. As a result, they and the children were able to create collaborative programs to improve the youths' lives, reintegrate them into society, reduce their unacceptable behaviors, and improve their communities in general (Tyler, F. B., Tyler, S. L., Echeverry, & Zea, 1991).

A somewhat comparable example arose in 1991. I was at a university in India on a Fulbright research fellowship. By then, my wife had obtained a graduate degree in anthropology and was doing research on domestic violence. We met with the female professors in the psychology department where I was in residence to explore the possibility of collaborating to study this sensitive topic. As members of the upper caste, the professors argued vehemently that women from lower caste families would never discuss such issues because of fear of retaliation from their husbands and mothers-in-law. My wife persisted, and we suggested that they accompany us on a visit to a fertility control clinic. Much to the professors' surprise, the village women spoke quite freely about their lives, including domestic violence. Further, they had firm ideas about their own roles in that violence and how they handle it. These female faculty changed their minds and decided to collaborate with my wife on that study. It provided very informative results about the strengths and active roles of Indian women in managing their lives and families (Tyler, S. L., Tyler, F. B., Dhawan, Punetha, & Sinha, 1996). The limitation of these high caste women's definition of other community women had kept them from seeing the full humanity of lower caste women, despite being psychology professors interested in women's issues.

These two vignettes are representative of any number of situations I have encountered. Both anecdotes show how our efforts to understand and interact with others in constructive ways are often hindered by our inability and/or our unwillingness to acknowledge our own biases and limitations. Unfortunately, although the failure to be open to the perspectives of others often stems from a narrowness of outlook rather than conscious intent, it makes us incapable of crediting others with strengths and resourcefulness. Over the years, these kinds of experiences have broadened my disciplinary perspectives and fed my interest in understanding how we can put together our lives and communities in ways that will enable us to live peaceably and join in providing for the well-being of everyone.

I have spent over a half-century as a psychologist, community activist, and government official engaged with individuals, disadvantaged groups, privileged groups, and communities. In some ways this book is a summary of my beliefs that have grown out of these experiences. That is, I believe that we need to consider ourselves and the individuals with whom we work as being responsive to our social environment (the community) and also consider the environment as being responsive to each of us. These individual/environment interactions generate essential dynamics either for nurturing human potential (i.e., a prosocial community that generates prosocial individuals) or for diminishing human potential (i.e., an anti-social community that generates antisocial individuals). To focus only on the individual or the community is to miss the transformation process of individuals and communities impacting each other as they create the experience of life.

When focusing on individuals it is of value to remember that we each develop a form of psychosocial competence that is appropriate for our situation, i.e., it is *ethnically valid*. When our situation changes either because of our actions or independently of us, we need to develop a new, psychosocial competence configuration that is ethnically valid for the new context. Reciprocally, when we focus on the contexts of our lives including our communities, we need to focus on understanding how they are organized. I have found that the structure and functioning of communities can be conceptualized as having a three-aspect form. *Social action* refers to the activities of civic leaders who formulate community policies. *Social planning* refers to the activities of professionals and intermediate level managers who contribute their specific expertise in carrying out social policies. *Locality development* refers to the individual and combined activities of residents to conduct their lives and resolve common problems. For a community or a larger society to function prosocially, the people in them must evolve ways of coordinating these three factors so that they serve their individual and collective interests. This three-level framework is a central theme in my work and throughout this book. It is presented in detail in Chapter 2.

To function effectively, societies must include a network of prosocial communities that maintain its coherence and constructively resist the divisive forces found among individual members and within each community. Societies must also manage relationships with outsiders, and embrace the community's commitment to the ongoing process of success, failure, and growth. In summarizing the past half-century of research on intercultural relations and nation building, Segall, Dasen, Berry, and Poortinga (1999) noted that in-groups tend to become ethnocentric over time. However, they stressed that available data also support that such an outcome is not inevitable. Overarching identities can be formed and ethnocentric-based conflict can be reduced when people's cultural similarities are emphasized and their proximity and opportunities for equal status contact are increased. Further, "when individuals locate themselves in a relatively small collectivity that has meaning as an in-group they can probably also identify comfortably with a larger collectivity that includes the smaller one" (Segall et al., 1999, p. 295).

That is, when people can maintain a personal identity in a small community, they seem to have also developed the base they need for forming a secure identity within a larger and more complex community. However, whether small communities can integrate with and be accepted by larger communities rests on whether doing so is seen to serve prosocial purposes for both. For example, in the United States today, the large culture-defining Anglo population of adults is being faced with the influx of a large contingent of immigrants from nearby Latin American countries. The survival of communities and the country itself rests on whether this decreasingly dominant majority can see personal and societal benefits in joining in overarching prosocial allegiances with this growing minority.

To undertake the task of broad, comprehensive change needed to create the prosocial communities that are such an essential element in our survival as individuals and societies, we have to formulate a definition of *community* that will be adequate for our purposes. That is not an easy or self-evident task. For example, in their dedication of *The Handbook of Community Psychology*, the editors, Rappaport and Seidman (1999) say "For our children and grandchildren *May you always live in a loving community where justice matters, where fairness and authenticity abounds and where the streets are filled with the joys of life, of learning, and of laughing" (1999, p. v)*. Yet ironically, in the Handbook they did not define a "loving community". They have left us wondering what such a community is and how to create or sustain one.

1.2. Defining a Prosocial Community

To answer this basic question about the definition of prosocial communities we have to understand the different natures and roles of the communities in our lives. We have to start by examining how we understand communities, beginning with our everyday sense of them as recorded in our dictionaries. The common meanings of *community, social,* and *well-being* used here are from the Random House

Webster's Collegiate Dictionary (1999). Even though these definitions are derived from and embedded in Western cultural concepts, they describe general patterns of relationships rather than any particular details of those relationships. Therefore, they give useful parameters for understanding what these terms mean in other cultures as well. Further, the adapted psychological definitions of these and other relevant terms will also be discussed as they become relevant throughout this text. The definition of *prosocial community* is mine and has grown out of my research and experiences. I have not been able to find either a dictionary or professional definition.

A *community* is defined as "a group of people who reside in a specific locality, share government, and often have a common cultural and historical heritage" (Random House, 1999). This definition focuses on the ties that provide a basis for community members to define themselves as a *group*. Their ties include the sharing of some set of rules (i.e., government) for living in close proximity as well as other social relationships. In a broad sense, Singer (2002) noted that due to globalization, the entire world has become a community. Thus we use the term community to refer to all kinds of groups starting with our families and extending out globally.

One problem with the dictionary's definition is that it does not address whether a community's members at any level share any common concerns for each other. We are left with incomplete information for making decisions about others in other communities, even though we know that differences exist. Unfortunately, the dictionary definition's omission also is characteristic of how communities are discussed in much of the professional and scientific literature. Dr. Rhodes (personal communication, October 13, 2006) indicated that in parts of the Arabic world, one's community is identifiable sociologically by observing those who can intermarry, the nature of their funeral ceremonies, and the places where people are buried. Knowing this, we can understand that in the Middle East eligibility to share life in this world and the hereafter imply a common concern, not just shared government and proximity. His definition also tells us that people's common concerns become a part of their identity - they give a reference of belongingness.

Based on experience, I have added these elements to my definition of community. To begin to address the role of *social* relationships in a community we have to add that dimension to our definition. Social is defined as "pertaining to, devoted to, or characterized by friendly companionship or relations" (Random House, 1999). Adding social to the concept of community adds the element of amicable, interpersonal relationships among the community's members. Even so, it only partially specifies the nature of the relationships involved. That is, we know that community relationships are not always or only amicable. Thus, this dictionary definition still lacks some major components needed for specifying the characteristics of effective, prosocially oriented community work.

Well-being is a psychosocial concept with a distinctive meaning when used in a prosocial community context. It involves both individual and social concerns. The dictionary's definition is silent about whether well-being is an individual or a psychosocial characteristic. It states only that well-being is "a good or satisfactory condition of existence; a state characterized by health, happiness, and prosperity; welfare" (Random House, 1999). In my work, I have expanded that definition so that well-being includes good or satisfactory internal relationships with oneself, external relationships with other individuals inside and outside of the community, and relationships with other relevant communities. It means feeling good about one's self, one's life, one's neighbors and neighborhoods, one's community, and about the world beyond. That same description of well-being can be applied to a community. A community can be thought of as providing a sense of well-being when it maintains the conditions and institutions that support people who thrive and who invest in others to help them thrive as they sustain and enrich the quality of life and relationships in the community.

With these ideas in mind, I define a *prosocial community* as one in which *everyone is committed to working together for their own well-being, each other's well-being, and that of the community, the society, and ultimately the world.* It is a community in which the people have a sense of collective responsibility for each other and for the community itself. This definition does not imply that there are no self interests, disagreements, or conflicts among community members. Instead, it stresses the primacy of everyone's felt need to preserve the community over more self-centered or even destructive forces.

Some community members try to exclude others; other members try to excuse themselves from carrying out their common responsibilities. Self-focused behaviors are core factors that create the dissensions and conflicts that arise within and between communities. A prosocial community is organized and functions so that no one becomes totally dominant and no one is ultimately defeated, excluded, or destroyed because of such conflicts. Rather, such communities survive and thrive by their investment in ongoing self-renewal. A particularly vital example of efforts to create a prosocial world is seen in the heightening social and political struggles over the world-wide threats of atmospheric pollution and global warming. Those threats not only transcend the scope of concern for existing communities and countries, they necessarily focus on and require a worldwide, coordinated prosocial response.

These definitions give us a starting place from which to explore the nature of prosocial communities. They lead to two of the basic sets of questions about the roles and relationships of individuals in such communities. First, how and to what extent are individual well-being and the well-being of the community interrelated? For example: To what extent should poverty bother me when no one whom I know is affected by it? After all, the more resourceful and affluent I am, the less I need community supports. Why should I get involved? How do I realize that the community needs my support? The second set of questions relate to how agreements, differences, and conflicts between individuals are to be understood and managed in each of their interests, their relationship with outsiders, individually and collectively, and the community as a whole. Answers to both types of questions are central in determining whether and how prosocial communities can be developed and sustained.

1.3. Characteristics of a Prosocial Community

If we want to create prosocial communities, having a definition is only the starting place. If we are to understand how prosocial communities function, we need to know their major characteristics and how they affect people's individual and collective behaviors. Those crucial components include: *Freedom, Unifying Functions, Complexity, The Community's Requirements, Human Dignity, and Individual Prosocial Morality* (conscience).

1.3.1. Freedom

In an earlier text (Tyler, F. B., 2001), I discussed how people's self-conceptions changed as the European world emerged from feudalism. In particular, as households and traditional community structures grew less deterministic of the individual's role, it became increasingly possible for people to behave autonomously and form a self-contained identity. The related concepts of autonomy and freedom continued to evolve, and individual rights have assumed a huge significance in today's world. Questions about the limits of freedom in relation to reciprocal relationships have also emerged and become focal concerns.

Particularly in Western countries, individual freedom is considered to have primacy over people's commitments to others and society. Consequently, we have lost the potential for public acceptance of the idea that everyone has a collective co-responsibility for the maintenance and development of their communities and societies. We seem to forget that people are necessarily psychosocial. Since everyone's identity and autonomy are formed in a social context, it is impossible for individuals to assume an autonomous status. Every individual needs a minimum of biopsychosocial support and socialization by adult caretakers–usually a family–and a broader social context, involving at least some form of community. For example, societies place limits on and teach new members what are considered acceptable public and private behaviors such as those related to gender, sexuality, violence, and the uses of the physical world.

To counter the societal emphasis on freedom and provide a balance that incorporates people's commitments to each other and society, the political philosopher, Selbourne (2001), argued for the primacy of the *civic order* as maintained by a *civic bond.* That bond is defined as:

> The ethic, voluntarily assumed but sustained by law and shared by the individual members of the civic order – to whatever community they may belong – which, governing the relations between individuals *qua* [as] citizens, dictates to and teaches such citizens that they compose a single civic order, whether of nation or city, to which they are affiliated and bound by the principle of duty, and for whose well-being they are responsible in their common interest. (Selbourne, 2001, pp. 19–20)

His underlying point is that we are born into this civic order, this set of rules, whose aim is to provide for individual and community survival and well-being. We are not born with "dutiless rights" (Selbourne, p. 59). Our continued survival and well-being require that we take as our primary duty the maintaining and enhancing of that civic order. It is also our primary duty to act to correct the civic order when it is corrupted and no longer serves its original purposes.

Selbourne (2001) presented his position as a necessary challenge to the more widely expressed assumption that each of us is born free, that is, entitled to our rights with no reciprocal responsibilities to contribute to the survival and well-being of the community's civic order. In his view, no society can flourish if its citizens consistently seek maximal individual freedoms and contribute to their community's survival only what is necessary to provide for their individual desires. Any community thus based on the primacy of individual freedom will inevitably end in civic disaggregation and fail as a society. There is no freedom without limits. For example, if no one in the community contributes to public education except to advance his/her personal interests, the society will not have an adequate educational system nor will it have educated people committed to sustaining it. Therefore, it is essential for any community's survival that its citizens continue to define how and to what extent individual freedom will be both guaranteed and contained.

1.3.2. Unifying Functions

Prosocial communities include intrinsic and extrinsic arrangements for people's individual and collective responsibilities and commitments to respect and provide for their own and each other's well-being along with that of the community in general. Their citizens bear a responsibility to address the need for social changes such as providing for adequate housing needed to restore, maintain, or advance the community's prosocial nature. That responsibility is embodied in civic obligations such as paying taxes, participating in the public dialogue, and obeying laws and other sanctions established to foster public welfare. A prosocial community also fosters an *intrinsic* sense of shared identity, worth, and caring among its members. It is often evidenced in our collective expressions of affection, honor, and grief or voluntary expressions of respect and affection for cherished people within a neighborhood community, an entire country, or even occasionally throughout the world. These celebratory actions acknowledge people's dignity as well as their autonomy, prosocial sense of relatedness, and duty to others. Community members also signify their commitment for both intrinsic and extrinsic reasons as active participants in the ongoing, prosocial process of creating, sustaining, and enhancing their community. They do so by participating in formally sanctioned rituals honoring their community as well as in the way they conduct their lives.

I previously (Tyler, F. B., 2001) identified and have reiterated here that a central characteristic of prosocial communities is people's concern and involvement with the well-being of others, the community, and themselves. This idea seems simple enough, but even existing societal institutions that are thought to be prosocial often tend to fall short of meeting that standard. For example, communities contain educational, economic, and social organizations to serve specific societal purposes. Educational institutions provide needed perspectives and skills to members of the community. However, they also filter out citizens who do not fulfill the expected requirements for becoming community members, or, once admitted, do not meet the performance criteria.

Some individuals may not be acceptable to any of the society's organizations, so they become marginalized, socially invisible, and/or face discrimination from the community. They are left to choose whether to remain as outsiders, act in non-socially sanctioned ways to change society so they can be included, or act against the community to maintain themselves and their identities (Tyler, F. B., 1973). Prosocial communities are designed to minimize these negative kinds of possibilities and behaviors. They provide guidelines for people to determine whether their ways of conducting themselves, forming relationships, and building their communities are acceptable. They also specify how to redress unjustifiable inequities once they have been identified. For example, it is not prosocial to focus exclusively on helping a disempowered group to become empowered, or help a privileged group to maintain their privileges without regard to the consequences for others.

Creating and maintaining prosocial communities requires substantial balancing of the complex considerations that arise for individuals and their contexts. For example, there is substantial evidence to support that integrating culture-defining (CDG) and non culture-defining (NCDG) students is beneficial to both and to the community at large. However, major problems exist in the United States because many, particularly among the CDG, have argued that providing relief from unequal educational opportunities for non-White students does not protect the assumed rights of the White students as based on past practices. There has been much less attention paid to emphasizing the advantages that integrated schools could have for both groups. This problem is not unique to the United States. Similar conflicts have arisen and persist in India and other countries over integrating lower caste or other ethnically devalued students into the educational system, the public civil service, and full participation in their societies.

In the field of community psychology, some have advocated for addressing the needs of disadvantaged individuals and groups, at times in ways that seem adversarial in relation to more advantaged individuals or segments of society. Nelson, Prilleltensky, and MacGillivary (2001) proposed that community psychologists should join with oppressed group members to address their needs. Such an approach by itself is not congruent with the goal of creating a prosocial community. The needs of the oppressed should be addressed, but not by acting against oppressors without regard to their justifiable needs. Emphasis is better placed on the potential benefits to both and the community if the oppressors become part of creating a prosocial community rather than remaining exclusionary. Both advantaged and disadvantaged people need to be informed that when they include everyone, it will also be to their benefit. By definition, a prosocial community's members are concerned about justice for everyone, not just the oppressed or the oppressors. Selbourne (2001) specifically argued that favoring any individuals or groups, such as the advantaged or disadvantaged, begins to disaggregate society, thus failing to meet this core objective. A prosocial community necessarily works toward the unification of its disparate groups and perspectives.

1.3.3. Complexity

The remains of historic and even prehistoric human habitations have characteristics of communities similar to ours of today. The first and most intimate of those communities is the family. It nurtures us from the beginning of our lives. In turn, the family is nested in an increasingly complex network of additional types of organized communities that transcend the roles of the individuals within them. Examples of such organizations include institutionally sanctioned structures such as schools, religious institutions, and governments. Their respective characteristics both enlarge and restrict the scope of our lives as each one influences the development of our characteristics and possibilities. We learn to negotiate the demands of each group we are involved with and thus often become as complex as the situations we respond to and the environments where we live.

1.3.4. The Community's Requirements

Any discussion of prosocially and antisocially oriented individuals and communities must begin with values. Values are the individual standards that we have chosen out of our personal, philosophical, religious, or other belief systems. Consequently, both the empirical evidence that characterizes scientific facts and the intuitive or faith-based values of non-scientific belief systems come, to some extent, from unverifiable propositions. The best that anyone can do is make his/her values and justifications as explicit as possible. The following sections highlight some major requirements whose resolutions are crucial in determining whether our communities will be prosocial.

1.3.4.1. Primacy (Civic Order and Co-responsibility)

Selbourne (2001), writing from the perspective of political philosophy, argued that without duty we do not have a civilized society. That is, unless people make a primary commitment to maintain a civic order (an organized social unit with shared obligations), they have no basis established for claiming privileges or rights. The rights of the community as a holistic unit must be supported and protected just as rights of individuals are. By collectively fulfilling our obligations to sustain the community, we also provide the context for exercising freedom and claiming personal rights. To fulfill our obligations requires that we defer or sacrifice some of our individual interests. Otherwise stated, unless individuals choose to honor their obligations, they cannot exercise their rights. The community will not include a means to honor their claims. In particular, those who are privileged or have otherwise been especially benefitted must honor their obligations to the community and to its disadvantaged residents. Unless they do, they have no grounds for expecting the community and the disadvantaged to honor them or respect their rights.

1.3.4.2. Scope

As noted earlier in this chapter, the term *community* refers to relationally integrated groups. Those groups range from families to ethnic, occupational, and ideological (religious, etc.) groupings to cultures and nation states. However, no matter how small or large or how the people in it are related, no community group is automatically prosocial. Segall et al., (1999) indicated that building prosocial communities at the level of small units is important, if not essential, for forming the conditions necessary to create larger prosocial units. Further, in any context, communities of different sizes and complexities are internested. Their natures and relationships to each other contribute to the issues they confront or create and to their level and quality of functioning. Communities also have a range of autonomy; they can function in distinctive ways without changing their relationships to other communities. For that reason if no other, it is important to consider communities and individuals as separate entities who are simultaneously in a symbiotic relationship to each other.

1.3.4.3. Context

No matter what its scope, a community and its people are influenced by their external environment. That external environment along with the community's internal environment (how it is organized and functions) provides the context that, in part, defines its possibilities and limits. All communities must respond to the limits of their resources for addressing the individual and collective needs and desires of their members. They must also respond to how those needs and desires interact with those of other communities.

Individual and group tensions have often been depicted in Western-based cultural dialogues as being pitted against each other (Christopher, Nelson, & Nelson, 2003). An overused but very relevant metaphor is that of a community with a Commons, an area owned collectively by members of that community for grazing animals. A tension arises from the fact that it is to the short term benefit of each community member to use that grazing area for as many animals as possible. However, if everyone takes that approach the commons will be destroyed, and everyone will lose access to that resource. This model assumes that people are motivated only by their own self-interest, have the unlimited right to behave accordingly, and that their individual and social concerns are independent of each other. The basic assumption is that people's freedom to use a common resource is independent of their commitment to their prosocial society's need to preserve the commons for the long term benefit of everyone.

Reasoning from this indefensible premise and from its logical conclusion that two goals or values cannot be maximized at the same time, leads to another incorrect conclusion, i.e., that either freedom or justice must be compromised to prevent the destruction of the commons. But, individual and social concerns are not independent of each other. People have discretionary choice capabilities; they can act like active agents and free themselves from the limiting effects of their histories and the self-destructive aspects of their natures (such as self-interest, narrowly defined). Reason and desire (facts and values) are not independent; they are contingent on each other and change with time and circumstances. Overall, individual and community resources are not independent over time; consequently, solving the Commons problem to the mutual benefit of both is possible. There are ways to reconceptualize these individual/community relationships so that they can be resolved prosocially.

1.3.4.4. Prosocial Justice

A pervasive concern in human affairs is the need to mediate conflicts in ways that preserve and satisfy the interests of the individuals and the community. Within the formal and informal social justice frameworks in most of the civilized world, resolutions of issues are considered to be "just" only when they meet the prosocial fairness and equatability criteria of both the community and the individuals involved. Tyler, T. R., Boeckman, Smith, and Huo (1997) formulated a social justice perspective on the basis of a United States-based experimental, social psychology paradigm and empirical data. They documented that individual and societal justice outcomes are intricately interconnected by showing the social consequences of individual decisions. They added that because of the individualistic focus of United States society and its social and behavioral sciences, the impact of its formal justice processes on the community's well-being has been largely ignored in favor of social justice for individuals. Specifically, conceptions of social justice are based on whether an involved person's outcome is considered fair or unfair by community standards, not by whether the outcome serves justice for the community (see Table 1.1 for justice standards and procedures). If we want to strengthen our communities, we must also ensure that outcomes are fair to them, thereby also strengthening the community.

Injustices emerge because of the inherent tensions that are part of social life, and justice is guided by social rules. However, justice is also based on the assumption and demonstrated fact that people have some choice about how they behave. Attaining justice requires balancing considerations among equality (each

TABLE 1.1. Justice standards and processes.

Concept	Term	Definition
Justice Standard	Relative deprivation	Is situation different from what it would be if standards of justice were applied?
Justice Processes	Procedural justice	Were fair procedures used to determine what is just in a situation?
	Distributive justice	Is each person provided what is deserved in contentious situations of unfairness?
	Retributive justice	Is a measure equal to the harm they did being done to violators of social standards?

Note: From "Social Justice in a Diverse Society", by T. R. Tyler, R. J. Boeckman, H. J. Smith, and Y. J. Huo, 1997, by Westview Press receiving the same), need (relative needfulness for finite resources), and equity (reward for merit). A prosocial community imposes the limitation that no one is granted complete domination or assigned complete rejection; justice for the community is also included in that equation. How to strike such a balance and whether existing approaches even envision doing so are crucial issues to the development and perpetuation of prosocial communities. Addressing these issues also involves identifying each community's concept of *prosocial* justice and considering that it may not be the same in all other communities or societies. As always, the issue of diversity arises as does the issue of freedom, i.e., how much any one person has a right or obligation to unilaterally define the reality of others and impose their perspectives on others.

1.3.5. Human Dignity

Dignity is a concept that is not always acknowledged as relevant in psychological accounts. When used as part of the term "human dignity" it denotes the idea of human worthiness apart from any specifiable utilitarian criterion. That is, it means that individuals have an intrinsic value, and in some irreducible sense, each is equally worthy of respect and consideration. Dignity is not something that children earn or can be granted or withheld by adults. Rather, it is an inherent part of being a human. Individuals or groups in power such as authority figures, culture-defining group members, or parents may use their power to try to deny or suppress children's senses of dignity, but they cannot ultimately destroy it. Ennew underscored that the key concept in human rights is "human dignity" (2002, p. 13). She stressed that honoring the belief that children have human rights requires that we acknowledge their dignity and consequent entitlement to participate in discussions about their lives.

Once children are allowed to participate in relevant decision making, adults will learn how much those children can contribute to their wider society. Stark (1992) reported on a project in Munich, Germany, in which adults and children worked together to plan and increase safe play opportunities. This approach led to significant improvement in the status of children and their sense that their dignity was acknowledged, even though problems arose when leading politicians opposed some of their suggestions and rejected their contribution.

Not only are children often denied their human dignity and their right to participate in issues that affect them, but that denial is also often directed at adult members of devalued groups. Although people vary in their capabilities, everyone can assume some level of responsibility for their own conduct and their contribution to their communities. We give credence to the evidence that people have discretionary capabilities of judgment and choice only when we honor their sense of dignity and respect their choices. Only when we have granted dignity to all community members can we create and maintain a sense of justice within a community. Finally, the community itself needs to have a sense of dignity and respect and be treated accordingly; otherwise, the community's role as provider and nourisher of its citizens will be undermined.

1.3.6. Individual Prosocial Morality (Conscience)

Each individual's internalized conception of his/her responsibilities is usually referred to as *conscience*. That inner sense is an essential component of any human agency. Consequently, it is important to consider how one's inner sense is formed and what determines whether it will include constructive prosocial characteristics or be limited to self-centered and other destructive characteristics.

Kochanska (2002) reported on the concept of a *mutually responsive orientation* (MRO) between mothers and children as having a positive impact on the development of prosocial consciences in children (although he does not use those words). His work and that of his colleagues focused on the mother-child relationship from early in life into the school age years. They defined MRO as "a positive, close, mutually binding, and cooperative relationship, which encompasses two components: *responsiveness* and *shared positive affect*" (p. 192).

Their extensive correlational and longitudinal studies found a direct relationship between the presence of an MRO initiated by the mothers between themselves and their children and the development of a strong prosocial conscience in their children and themselves across a wide range of contexts. Kochanska's (2002) analyses indicated that this effect was a product of at least two mechanisms. An MRO promoted a more positive, happy mood in the children and, in turn, an eager, responsive stance toward following their mother's lead. These positive relationships were thought to influence the mothers and their children to form internal representations described as a "working model of a cooperative, reciprocal, mutually accommodating relationship in which partners naturally do things for one another without abrogating their autonomy" (Kochanska, p. 104). Kochanska emphasized that not just mothers, but other members of the family and the broader environment influence the child's development, although much remains to be learned about their effect. These findings provide a solid indication of the kinds of psychosocial dynamics that are relevant to whether and how people and communities develop prosocial orientations.

At present the idea that a mutually responsive orientation is or results in a prosocial conscience is tentative and needs far more validation. Even so, it encapsulates the sense of a basic integration of the autonomy and relatedness aspects of our relationships to ourselves, others, and society. It asserts that we need not consider that our sense of loyalty to our own integrity and to that of our relationships with others is separate and/or in opposition. We can be true both to ourselves and to others. The two can be fused with benefits going to us and to our relationships. That is at least a tentative formation of what having a prosocial conscience can mean.

Each person's conscience is established within and is a vital element in our agency. To make choices is to be an active agent and includes making choices about the nature and content of our consciences. As Koshanska (2002) demonstrated, conscience is a product of our milieu including our interpersonal relationships as well as our individual experiences. People are not necessarily self-centered in a narcissistic way; they may be self-centered in a shared prosocial way. A sense of prosocial integrity can extend to our family and beyond to our neighborhood, our country, and even to humanity.

1.4. Studying and Intervening in Communities

Throughout history, self-appointed as well as professionally appointed change agents have assumed their right to study or intervene in communities to accomplish particular objectives. They frequently do not consider that their sojourn will be influenced by the resident community's understanding of its own interests and possibilities. Change agents will not be successful unless they consider or attempt to understand the complexity of the community and of their own roles in it whether they impose themselves by force and military conquest or seek entry with presumed benevolent intent and a sense of superior knowledge and values.

It is difficult to create a relationship between community members and investigators or change agents that is mutually acceptable and worthwhile for everyone. The participants must identify each other's interests, and in particular, the role that the outsiders want to assume within the community. A central issue needing clarification is the nature of the ways the outsiders are–and in what ways they are not–members of the community. The community and the change agents must then establish which types of mutually beneficial relationships can be formed.

Changing any community also brings changes to at least some aspects of its environment and its relationships to other communities. Consequently, questions arise about the responsibilities of the outside agents and those in the community about their impact on the surrounding environment and neighboring communities. For example, how will damming a stream to create a lake in a park impact on downstream areas? Unfortunately, such questions can be extended into an infinite regress, so practical limits must be established or nothing can be accomplished. However, such concerns and their relationship to other criteria need to be considered by anyone who wishes to intervene in communities.

In the long run, constructing a prosocial society is impossible unless each segment of the society will be better served. Pickren and Tomes (2002) quoted from the first meeting of the Board of Social and Ethnic Responsibility for Psychology (about the consequences of getting the American Psychological Association involved in social justice issues) "to turn one's social and ethical questions on oneself will necessarily create conflict" (Pickren & Tomes, p. 51); that is, those committed to change must first consider the implications for themselves. They must also be willing to change themselves before they can establish a framework needed to create prosocial communities. For example, there are towns in the United States that were built around a labor source such as a factory. In subsequent years, the factory may have been sold to a large corporation which subsequently decided to close it because the profit margin was too low. In a number of those towns, the local residents, businesses, and institutions banded together to buy the factory and manage it themselves. A major factor in the success of those efforts has been whether the factory workers and factory manager become active, collaborative participants in managing this enterprise. In contrast, if the workers had simply hired a factory manager and continued in their roles as workers doing their daily job and then going home, the factories were likely to fail. In these so-called *employee owned companies*, success was likely only if the workers and the town reformed themselves as a kind of prosocial community (Quarrey & Rosen, 1994).

The most seminal figure in psychology's struggle is Kenneth B. Clark. He and his wife conducted research that showed how racism impacted on the psychosocial development of what were then called Negro and White children. Those findings became an integral part of the U. S. Supreme Court's 1954 decision to outlaw segregation in public schools. Clark was the first (and still the only) African-American president of the American Psychological Association. He contributed to changes in the APA, its policies, and its members through his contributions as a scholar and as a public policy figure. He was also a participant in the community of psychology faced with cleaning itself up internally and in its relationship to the broader community. In his own life, he was an exemplar of the struggle in his role as an "involved observer" and "participant-symbol" (Keppel, 2002). He used the colonialist metaphor to define the impact of context by writing that "the dark ghetto is *institutionalized pathology [*my italics*]*" (Clark, 1965, p. 34).

Creating prosocial communities requires broad integrated changes at levels ranging from societal structures and social policies to assumptions about the rights of individuals and their responsibilities to others and to the societies in which they live. Joining prosocial ideas and practices is essential for us if we are to experience the insights that foster our paradigmatic shifts. More specifically, creating prosocial communities rests on eliminating conceptions and mechanisms that exclude groups or individuals. It then builds by creating other conceptions and mechanisms that include all groups and individuals. Finally, it depends on each of us in our complex individual and organizational identifications, affiliations, and actions to apply these same requirements to ourselves and participate as part of that process, not separate from it. I have intentionally avoided saying that creating a prosocial community *requires* these attributes and activities. Prosocial communities can not rest solely on requirements. In the final analysis, they are created by and sustain their existence only through the voluntary commitments of their members to an overarching goal.

Stating these broad requirements and objectives is relatively easy in comparison to the task of actually spelling out the steps required to accomplish them. The rest of this text is focused on that task. Its goal is to present a comprehensive conceptually integrated Transcultural Ethnic Validity Model to guide efforts to understand and implement the kinds of reciprocal changes in communities and the people living within them to facilitate their movement toward becoming a prosocial community.

2
Psychosocial Integration: The Theoretical Framework

Each of us plays an active role in creating our communities and deciding what kinds of communities will best serve our interests. We are also shaped by our experiences in those communities along with our other unique personal experiences. My colleagues and I (Tyler, F. B., 2001) have developed a two-faceted, interlocking framework for studying these ideas. The two facets are, respectively, (1) ourselves behaving as active agents, and (2) the environments within which we function. The empirical evidence supporting them is presented in detail in my earlier text (2001). My objective in this chapter is to describe this conceptually integrated account of each of those facets, the individual and the environment, and of how they are interrelated.

The aspect of that framework concerned with how we function as individuals is called a *Transcultural Ethnic Validity Model* (TEVM). We act within our personal life spaces as individuals, and we also act with others to organize the communities where we live (Tyler, F. B., 2001). Those two types of actions are often thought of as separate, although they affect each other in profound psychological as well as other ways. The basic thesis of this book is that there is a way to organize ourselves and our communities that will provide us with an individual and collective supportive and nurturing quality of life. This chapter provides an integrated framework for understanding ourselves, our communities, and the influence each has on the other so that we can bring about prosocial changes. This second model is called the *Prosocial Community Model.*

2.1. Transcultural Ethnic Validity Model

The core idea of the Transcultural Ethnic Validity Model (TEVM) is that individuals are socialized and develop their characteristic styles of living and functioning within a sociocultural milieu. Relying on that model can help us better organize and influence our own conduct so that we can promote our well-being and that of others inside and outside of our social units. The model involves three, interrelated components, namely: (a) a *Psychosocial Competence Model* for describing how people organize their lives in view of their context and situations, (b) the *Ethnic*

Validity patterns that describe how individuals acquire the ways to live that are appropriate within their context, and (c) the *Nested Framework* nature of people's environments. The TEVM gives us a way to understand these processes, i.e., it is a model that, to a major extent, represents the societal organization within which people are born and live out their lives. The TEV model incorporates the shared patterns of an entire ethnic group or society as well as the unique variant of that pattern which each of us personally constructs. Further, if we keep our own patterns and the shared patterns of our social group in mind as we work to understand and change ourselves along with our social units, we will be better able to provide supportive contexts for everyone else's constructive prosocial development. Representative aspects of all of the components of this model and how they interrelate are described in the following sections.

2.1.1. A Hypothetical Example

In the following paragraphs, you will meet two hypothetical, young United States citizens, Alan and Beth. They will illustrate how the TEV model helps us explore the ways we all relate to each other's backgrounds, personal characteristics, and common situations. Alan and Beth also provide a way for us to understand how the TEV framework of their early experiences influence their later life roles in shaping the communities in which they will live and work. As we consider how they fit into various situations, we can gain a better understanding of how different situations incorporate Alan and Beth and whether they do so in a prosocial way. We can also see how the complex psychosocial individuality that each brings to these situations can have an impact on the situation or, in contrast, be suppressed or distorted by it.

Alan is a white male who attended a parochial grade school and public high school. He is a first-generation graduate of his large, urban, state university. His parents were born to poor families in a village in France. They met, married, and immigrated to the United States when they were young adults. They settled in Toledo, Ohio, and found work in blue collar service jobs to support their family and provide their children better opportunities in life than had been available for them. They taught their children the importance of working hard, supporting themselves, remaining faithful to their Roman Catholic religion, and getting ahead through their own efforts. Alan has worked for as long as he can remember, including during high school and college, and he still has a large student debt to repay. After his recent graduation, he applied for a publicly supported teaching position in an under served school in order to have part of his educational debt forgiven.

Beth is a black female graduate from an elite, private high school and an elite college for black students in Atlanta, Georgia. Her family has a history that includes slavery but has, for several generations, been part of the black, higher income, professional class. Beth's parents live in an affluent suburb of Atlanta, and both have professional careers. They taught her to be proud of her ancestry, strive to uphold their family traditions, follow the tenets of their African Methodist beliefs, and contribute to the well-being of her people. They paid for her education and provided her with enriched cultural experiences throughout her life. She applied for a publicly supported teaching position in an under served school to become better acquainted with youth, particularly black youth, who have had few advantages and to contribute to them before making any further decisions about her own future directions.

Alan's and Beth's lives cross paths when they are both assigned to the same inner-city high school in Washington, D.C. It has a majority of black students with a minority of white and Latino students. Some of the students are immigrants or first generation children of immigrants from a variety of countries. The faculty and staff reflect the student body in that the majority are black with varying numbers of Latino and white members from a range of social classes.

Alan and Beth have each formed psychosocially based ways of facing their lives that they bring to this new community. They both have been socialized in individualistic, United States society. We can expect that both should have acquired a sense of themselves as autonomous and in control of their life, as trusting of others and expecting benevolence in their world, and as having an active, organized way of solving their life issues. However, each of them has faced experiences which have made them question themselves in relation to that ideal–Alan because of his immigrant heritage, Beth because of her heritage as an African American. As colleagues in their new jobs, they will share the common task of learning how to be effective teachers in a dysfunctional and often hostile school community. It does not occur to them that when they meet and begin to interact with each other as teachers or as individuals, they will be faced with forming a shared (what I call transcultural) sense of ethnic validity. In a sense, they each need to participate in the formation of a new "community of two" if they are to have a basis for interacting. Further, they must each invest in their community for it to take on a prosocial character.

Transcultural exchanges are most evidently *transcultural* to us in such instances as a marriage between two people from different countries or as in the arrival of immigrant refugees who find a way to fit into their new country with its already formed community groups. In Alan and Beth's situation, even though they have both grown up in the United States, their exchanges will likewise have many of the same transcultural features as those between immigrants facing a new life situation. As they begin to work together, they will have to face the challenges and changes that accompany the formation of any new relationship or they cannot become friends or even develop a work relationship.

Alan and Beth understand and approach their teaching tasks with quite different expectations. Alan shares the experience of economic struggles that his new students are dealing with, particularly the experiences of the minority white students in the school. He had previously interacted minimally with some black students in school and college, although he did not seek to get acquainted with them. Alan was socialized to believe that it is ethnically valid for him to achieve beyond what his family and ancestors accomplished and to distance himself from the limits of their past. His choice to serve the less fortunate is to some extent, if not entirely, based on his strategy for self-advancement. In contrast, Beth and the black students share the common experience of facing racism, but she does not share their history of economic struggles. She has been socialized to know that an ethnically valid way of life includes honoring and building on the accomplishments of her ancestors while also serving the less fortunate in society, particularly African American people. The students are not likely to share her sense of advancement possibilities or her sense of past family accomplishments on which to build their futures. In fact, because of her privileges, they may resent her.

In terms of relating to each other, Alan has had limited experience with privileged members of society, no experience with an elitist college, and only minimal acquaintance with people from black communities. Beth has had at least limited experience with white professional colleagues or friends of her parents, but very little with poor, working class, black or white families. To form any kind of personal or collegial relationship, Beth and Alan have to build on shared, personal characteristics such as friendliness, or even the experience of participating in a shared training program. For their friendship to continue developing, they must begin to address their preconceived biases about each other and the inevitable misunderstandings that will arise during their various interactions due to their different heritages.

2.1.2. Individual Psychosocial Competence

We each form our own Individual Psychosocial Competence Configuration (PSC). It is the model within the TEV configuration that we use to represent our "selves". I use it to describe the integrated character of our conduct, that is, how we behave as individuals. Whether we refer to PSC as personality or identity or assign to it some other name, it is the unique and distinct center of our individuality and the perspective from which we view ourselves and the world. This term conveys my view that the core of individuality is each person's integrated ongoing way of organizing and conducting their lives. It is both a product of our natures and histories and a somewhat open-ended, discretionary outgrowth of our capacities to abstract, create meaning, and make choices. Our choices include how we define our sense of self-awareness and organize our approaches to planning and decision making.

At a common sense level, it is self-evident that people have agentic properties. However, psychologists often have trouble accepting the idea that people make judgments, that is, discretionary choices that are not totally predictable by what they know about themselves or others know about them. In my view, this decision making characteristic is as important to take into account as the social or bilingual determination of our thoughts and behaviors. For example, when individuals such as marginalized youth experience their community's rejection of them, they can respond by fighting main stream society or becoming part of it. Consequently, their capacity to choose becomes a factor in whether their community can become prosocial. However, the rest of us also make choices that can influence their decisions. Specifically, we can influence their thoughts and interest in participating in prosocial behaviors by providing them with experiences from which benefits come in response to cooperation.

Individual psychosocial competence refers to the broad, holistic formulation that we create to give ourselves an integrated viewpoint for organizing and testing our personal hypotheses about our own conduct and that of others. We also use it to guide how we conduct ourselves and interact with people. It includes the belief that we are part of the natural world and as such are products of our natures, circumstances, and experiences. We are also self-aware *knowers* who have some discretionary control over our own lives. We use our individual experiences to construct our lives, identities, and relationships to our contexts. However, since our private experiences occur in contexts whose meanings are somewhat socially constituted, we have a social as well as an individual character; that is, our experiences are psychosocial. Our individual experiences and their social contexts are not the same thing but we cannot describe either without reference to the other. Further, over time, we and our contexts continue to influence each other even as they continue to change in different ways.

People have capabilities for shaping both their personal destinies and their life contexts. We function as somewhat autonomous individuals and also as members of collectives and groups which are constrained by the natures, histories, and choices of all the members. The ways in which we evolve our psychosocial characteristics guide our participation in our own lives and in our communities. We are not fixed, unchanging entities; rather, we are all engaged in an ongoing process of both maintaining and changing our lives and our contexts. Because of this process, we need to conceptualize how we make those changes to understand ourselves, others, and our influences on each other.

The ways in which we organize our experiences and direct or change our lives can be conceptualized as involving three major, interrelated aspects. Specifically, we guide ourselves in relation to our understanding of our (a) *self attributes*, i.e., our sense of efficacy or control of the events in our lives, (b) *self-world attributes*, i.e., our relationships to our world and the others in it (that is, how much we feel others are trustworthy and to what extent we consider the world to be predictable and benign), and (c) *behavioral attributes*, i.e., how we organize our approach to managing the events in our lives. We frame these internal aspects of ourselves in relation to our external interactions in enormously complex ways. Since this text is focused primarily on forming prosocial communities, that complexity will be explored only briefly here to show how these aspects interrelate and influence the choices we make, including when we are creating communities.

2.1.2.1. Self Attributes

Within psychology's realm of personality theories and research, the major focus is and has been on people's presumed senses of discretionary choice and capacity for mastery over themselves and the events in their lives. These characteristics have variously been conceptualized as self-efficacy, personal control (of events and their outcomes), and assumption of responsibility for the events in one's life.

Self efficacy is usually accompanied by some degree of favorable to unfavorable self-evaluation. A belief in our own self efficacy is central to our conception of ourselves as *knowers* because it is based on the presumption that we have some discretionary capabilities for guiding our lives.

The conceptualization and study of this core attribute has produced an enormous body of psychological literature, most of it from a universalistic perspective (for summaries, see Lefcourt, 1984; Tyler, F. B., 2001). In general, the findings suggest that people with a more internal sense of control and/or stronger sense of self-efficacy learn more from their experiences. This result is particularly true when the outcomes of the events surrounding those experiences are thought to be amenable to skill rather than to chance and external control. However, some cross-culturally oriented studies have shown that psychosocial factors have an influence on a sense of self efficacy. They include gender, family and community composition, ethnicity (including racial attributions), social status, and biological makeup. Both the general effect of a person's self-efficacy and the particular contextual factors underlying it are important considerations that must be taken into account in the development of prosocial communities. Beth's social status has given her a strong sense of self-efficacy. If her teaching experience goes well, her sense of self-efficacy will probably grow. Alan has faced a more difficult struggle in building a solid sense of self-efficacy because of his marginal status as the child of immigrants and his childhood in a blue collar community. His sense of self-efficacy will also be strengthened if he becomes an effective teacher for these students, particularly the black students with whom he has previously had minimal experiences and little reason to believe in their capabilities.

2.1.2.2. Self-World Attributes

Most of us legitimately assume that the events in our lives and their outcomes are influenced by circumstances outside of ourselves. Out of our direct and vicarious experiences, we formulate expectations about how our world is likely to respond to our actions. We behave accordingly and experience varying degrees of success. As I have documented (Tyler, F. B., 2001), people who are at least moderately trusting and somewhat hopeful tend to behave more confidently and constructively and have more rewarding outcomes, particularly if they have lived in and continue to be in environments that are somewhat benign and predictable. In contrast, people who have lived in and may continue to live in threatening and unpredictable environments form distinctively different self-world attributes. They may develop hostile and/or other self-protective patterns which to them seem more appropriate to their circumstances. Unfortunately, such behaviors also often have destructive consequences as they increase stress levels and reduce opportunities for everyone to build prosocial relationships both within and outside of their immediate social units.

Beth probably grew up in a more benign and predictable environment than has been the case for the boys and girls who will be in her classes in the inner city school. They probably have considerably less reason to trust her than she has to trust them. Alan also probably had more support than the youth he is encountering or he would not have gone as far as he has in becoming their teacher. He has probably had more positive experiences with trust than they and so is in a better position to trust them than they are to trust him. In fact, these students may feel that neither Alan nor Beth really cares about them, but are there to teach in the high school as a step in the pursuit of their own long term goals. Alan and Beth will have to demonstrate that they do care about their students before they can successfully teach them anything, including teaching them how to be trusting.

When Alan and Beth meet their marginalized and suspicious students, they are all entering a new environment because they all bring their self-world expectations to that meeting. However, by organizing that environment and their interactions so that they are more benign and prosocially oriented, all of them can begin a spiral of prosocial behaviors. Alternatively, if they structure their interactions in hostile and threatening ways, they can start a downward spiral toward distrust and conflict.

2.1.2.3. Behavioral Attributes

Whatever our senses of our own efficacy and of the nature of our environment, we have to choose ways to handle our ongoing lives, even if we do so passively. That is, circumstances force us to respond in some way to the events that occur in our lives, whether caused by our own actions or by something outside of us. On the basis of our experiences over time, we construct a characteristic approach to engaging with life by initiating and responding to events. From my point of view, the origins, nature, and consequences of our behavioral attributes has received considerably less attention from professionals than it deserves. Much of the relevant research has been conducted under the rubric of coping with stress; those studies have shown that proactive approaches are crucial to dealing with stress effectively (Folkman & Moskowitz, 2004; Tyler, F. B., 2001).

Research over the past thirty years has demonstrated that a constructive, planful approach is necessary for people to effectively adapt to their life circumstances and their potential triumphs over difficulties under all circumstances. My own work has focused on the role of active, planful engagement with events during ordinary life as well as in relation to stressful events. I have found that active planful engagement may be even more important to constructive coping than is a sense of self-efficacy or trust for those who live in hostile and otherwise difficult circumstances. That is, actively addressing life's challenges is a more productive strategy than avoiding them or refusing to face them, even when in a hostile and unpredictable environment. Alan and Beth have learned the value of this kind of active organized approach in their own lives. They are now able to teach it to their students even though, or perhaps particularly because, those students face limited opportunities and live in environments that are both physically dangerous and psychologically destructive. How to use an organized approach to their lives as well as their studies is potentially the most important message Alan and Beth have to teach as well as model for these youth.

2.1.3. Ethnic Validity

We all have identities as individuals and as members of particular ethnic groups. In this sense, ethnicity has two meanings. The more general meaning describes ethnicity as membership in a specific group which shares a distinctive culture, religion, language, or other such characteristic. At this level, ethnicity describes the characteristics common to members of a culture or nation, and also of other groups of a more limited scope such as a community. Even the citizens of major civilizations have a shared sense of their ethnic validity, of what is a valid way of being a member of their civilization. Alan and Beth share a United States based ethnic validity and so will assume that many of the customs and traditions that they both follow are expected behaviors. Consequently, they expect to see them in each other.

A more limited meaning of ethnicity is that of membership in a minority or other societally designated and often devalued group which shares a distinctive culture or belief system and way of life within a larger society with a different ethnicity. This sub group may not be allowed equal status with the larger group nor may it wish to conform to the larger group's ethnic way of living. For example, it is ethnically valid for Beth to believe in and behave in accordance with the norms of her family and its African Americans customs and traditions. Similarly, it is ethnically valid for Alan as part of his family's background to behave according to their French norms as well as those of the United States. That is, for each of us, our reality and way of life has integrity and personal validity from the perspective of our particular nested framework's coherence and validity.

A more graphic example of a blended ethnic validity was related to me by an Italian American community worker. His large extended family had gathered at his parent's home for Thanksgiving dinner which, for most U.S. residents, is traditionally roast turkey. He and his brother got into an argument about whether their predominantly Italian American neighborhood should emphasize segregating itself within their multiethnic city or assimilating with other groups. Their mother eventually became exasperated, and closed the argument by saying, "We're all Americans. Sit down and eat your spaghetti."

At all levels, our ethnic validity is shaped by both the internal and external coherence of our contexts. Consequently, our prosocial ethnic validity within our own culture is also influenced by the ethnic validity and cultural coherence of the other subcultures around us. Thus, we define personal ethnic validity in relation to any number of overarching, transcultural ethnic validity conceptions. In its totality, this ethnic validity formulation is the nested framework within which we define and judge ourselves, others, and our reality. We construct and revise it out of our capabilities and our changing understanding of our experiences. This idea is highlighted in the following paragraphs.

Destiny refers to the many aspects of our lives and contexts over which we have little or no control. For example, our genetic makeup, life cycle, and the era and geographic social context in which we live are beyond our control. We may pine for our lost youth or wish we had been born in a different time and place, but these wishes can never become choices. Alan may eventually escape being an individual outside of the dominant culture because he can become completely assimilated to the white Culture Defining Group (CDG); Beth cannot escape her "outsider" heritage in the United States because her skin color clearly identifies her background, and she cannot change it. Her destiny would be quite different if she lived in a predominantly African culture. In either case, destiny must always be a consideration in any attempt we make to understand ourselves or others.

Our *histories* consist of the events of our accumulated personal and collective pasts. In the United States they are influenced, to a great extent, by the dominant white culture. Even though our personal experiences and those of the people with whom we directly and indirectly share our lives are separate from that dominant group, they are influenced by it. Our histories contribute to our dreams and fears as well as to many of the ways we approach each day and our overall lives. Some of Alan's fears may involve the threat of being denigrated as the son of immigrants. His dreams may focus on becoming assimilated to his new American context and achieving to a level above that which his parents accomplished. Beth seems likely to dream of finding a way to live that transcends, or at least avoids, racism while she also fears that her life will be diminished by it.

Continuity speaks to the ongoing consequences of our heritage as part of social groups and life contexts. As noted above, we are influenced by the varied histories of our ancestors. Their dislocations and transitions have changed the quality of their lives and/or their culture-defining status from generations past to the dreams of future generations. Thus, our heritages bring complex personal, community, and cultural meanings to our past, present, and projected futures. When Alan's parents immigrated to the U. S., their emphasis on breaking with the past created discontinuity in their family. Beth is marked by her socialization to be proud of the continuity embedded in her ancestors' ability to overcome their heritage of bondage and to build on that tradition. For the Maori of New Zealand, the answer to the question, "Who are you?", is a recitation of oneself plus all of one's ancestors and all of one's potential descendants (Nikora, Personal communication, October, 1994). For them, continuity defines identity. In contrast, for an individual in the United States, the answer to the question, "Who are you?", is a recitation of that person's unique qualities as separate from everyone else's. That is, for residents of the United States identity is defined as autonomy, the attribute mentioned below.

Autonomy focuses on that component of our thoughts, feelings, and actions that is often celebrated as freedom and mastery of one's fate. It, too, is socially, developmentally, and individually shaped. The personal meaning of freedom is constrained or expanded by our experiences and societal contexts and helps us understand that freedom has boundaries of all kinds. Perhaps necessarily, we occasionally think about whether and how freedom exists, what its true nature is, and to what extent and in what ways we are free. We also explore the relationship of our freedom in comparison to that of others, including whether we have any obligation to respect their freedom. Thus, being free and autonomous entails the ways and extent to which we assume discretionary choice in our lives. Both Beth and Alan have made particular kinds of choices in the way they want to live. Although these decisions will continue to have an impact and influence on their future choices, they can reinterpret and use their sense of freedom as an ongoing guide. Further, as applied to our societies, communities, or ethnic groupings, being free refers to the extent to which the context sets broad or narrow limits in individual or group behavior. Thus, we may speak of a *free* society in contrast to a closed society.

All of these ethnic validity factors interact to influence our societies and our lives at all levels. For example, the life experiences and meaning assigned to being a male or a female have certain basic commonalities across humanity. However, there are also very distinctive meanings created by each social group. A woman from the secular Western World forms an ethnically valid way of defining herself that is quite at odds with what is an ethnically valid way for a Muslim woman, particularly in the Middle East or Asia, to define herself. If at some later time, Beth were to travel to the Middle East to continue broadening her world view, but behaves and interprets others' behavior just as she would at home, nothing that she does will be ethnically valid to the people in this ethnically different setting. Her conduct will seem inappropriate to the women (and the men) in this new context due to its different ethnic validity rules, codes, and expectations. To function effectively and maintain a sense of ethnic validity, Beth will have to expand her framework and learn to manage both sets of expectations. That is, she will need to broaden her sense of transcultural ethnic validity so that it becomes more comprehensive. She will have to grasp that appropriate dress standards for work are context dependent. She can then understand and manage her familiar, Western ethnic validity conception of herself as going to work bareheaded and her new, Middle Eastern ethnic validity self-conception as wearing a head scarf to work. Conversely, if she continues to persist in her customary dress, the members of her new host group will be faced with choosing either a prosocial welcoming stance toward this diversifying experience for them or accept that she "doesn't understand" and let her be marginalized and ignorant of what she has missed.

The complexity of our lives and contexts is one of the major influences on how we construct our senses of ethnic validity. Large overarching groupings such as nations and cultures are made up of heterogeneous subgroups. The large groups are primarily defined by one of the prominent ethnic subgroups referred to as the *culture-defining group* (CDG). The CDG in the United States is the non-Latin European heritage white subgroup. Those who are socialized as part of the CDG generally live in a relatively benign and supportive context. In contrast, the people in the other subgroups of that culture are embedded in *non culture-defining groups* (NCDGs) and required to define themselves, conduct their lives, and evolve a life direction in a context where their primary identity is more or less devalued. Because they have to adapt to the larger CDG context, they live in a less benign and supportive world where their NCDG ethnic validity has to be adjusted to fit within the demands of the CDG model. Both Alan and Beth, though for quite different reasons, have had to form their senses of ethnic validity within their NCDG status. Alan's NCDG heritage as the child of recent immigrants has marginalized him; to an even greater extent, Beth's NCDG black heritage has marginalized her even more and in different ways from Alan's. The context of their new jobs will challenge both, and they will have to make further changes in their senses of ethnic validity.

2.1.4. Nested Frameworks

Mountains and oceans would presumably exist even if people did not. However, our *concepts* of mountains and oceans cannot exist separately from our symbolic labeling of them. That is, we individually and collectively identify a set of characteristics and use them to recognize, interpret, and understand particular ideas or objects. We then assign labels or names such as "culture", "ethnicity", "race", and "religion" to refer to those characteristics. Each term becomes a concept for framing how its members organize their society. Such terms and their meanings are constructed by people who individually and collectively incorporate them into their personal psychosocial frameworks for describing and explaining their experiences. The set of characteristics or concepts called a *nested framework* is crucial in enabling us to understand and explain the relationships that exist between ourselves and our social context and heritage.

When we use the term, *nested framework*, we are referring to the characteristics that we attribute to ourselves to explain how we organize and live our own distinctive lives. For example, in characterizing Alan and Beth I described their different sociocultural frameworks. The generalized nested framework of Black United States society is not exactly the same as Beth's personal one, but the two influence each other. The same is true for Alan in relation to White United States culture. Both their personal and social sets of frameworks will be influenced when they interact and even further when they interact with their students. Each has chosen to move beyond their historical contexts and explore new ways to live. They will continue to define and use their sense of freedom to guide their future lives. They will also continue to be influenced by the social networks of their pasts.

Our human capacity to abstract and construct meaning is a product of our natures as creatures with advanced, sophisticated, perceptive and cognitive capabilities. The process by which any of us abstracts meaning is to some extent unique and is referred to as the *personal equation*. This term comes from a long-ago verified finding that no two people can make exactly the same observation because no two individuals are exactly alike and no pattern of sensory input compels any particular formulation of meaning (Boring, 1929). We continuously construct and adapt our unique psychosocial realities. However, people with similar socialization experiences often report similar observations because they have learned to assign meaning to their experiences, in part through direct and vicarious tutelage from others. Further, people interact with those around them so that, over time, they modify their abstractions for many purposes in order to establish shared meanings. In sum, it is not possible for the patterns or levels of abstraction made by different people to be either identical or unrelated. For example, while Beth and Alan agree to a great extent with their respective parents about the nature of inner city schools, their teaching experiences will result in both of them modifying their original negative beliefs about such schools and their students. While they may change their beliefs in a more positive direction, they may or may not be able to convince their parents' to change their beliefs about either the schools or the students.

The most basic societal nested framework within which each person functions is that of the family which provides for essential nurturing and protection. That nurturing may be provided by the mother, the father, and/or other immediate family members, or all members may share or supplement each other's efforts. The family lives within the next more general framework of the nested configuration–that of a community, tribe, or other psychosociocultural unit made up of personal (biological, psychological, or other relatedness) and social ties. Those ties link the relationships of people in the unit to other units and their members. These linkages are formed in increasingly comprehensive ethnic, cultural, or other societally identified relationships to form an internested matrix. Within that matrix, people create and maintain their own somewhat distinctive psychosocial identities and guidelines for relating to others and their social units. For these reasons, Beth and Alan have quite distinct and different understandings and approaches to their new jobs. This teaching experience will add another set of frameworks to those they have already established.

There are, as part of our shared socialization experiences, organized belief/knowledge systems to which we are exposed throughout our lives. They contribute to the nature of the nested frameworks that we each construct, and they are important influences on how we understand ourselves, others, and the world around us. These shared, often tacit, ways of knowing reality by any community of people at a specific time are often referred to as common sense. However, from the perspectives of members of other groups, common sense is not common at all, or sometimes even sensible. To Alan, it is common sense to realize that each of us has to take care of him/herself. To Beth, it is common sense to expect people to be helpful to the less fortunate.

There are also frameworks of a different sort, such as those of religions and secular-based fields including the sciences, professions, arts, and humanities. These frameworks are intermingled with our nested societal frameworks. They give us additional ways to account for various aspects of our experiences that might otherwise be unresolvable. For example, religious systems provide ways for us to understand problems related to empirically unanswerable questions such as those of our ultimate origins, our futures beyond this life, and standards for social conduct. Religiously-oriented answers tend to be justified on the basis of faith; that is, they rest on untestable but societally accepted assumptions. However, empirical evidence shows us that religious answers are also derived from our personal experiences and social conditions.

Scientists use their specialized training and measurement tools to provide empirical evidence to determine specific answers to relevant questions. However, scientific fields also rest in part on untestable assumptions and on biases in their premises, constructions, and conclusions. Those aspects of scientific work are also shaped by individual and collective experiences and reliance on the socialization histories of the involved scientists. For example, Guttman (1977), an anthropologist who surveyed studies about the influence of cultural and gender differences in aging across the life span, concluded that psychologists could not begin to comprehend the complexity of such influences because they do not include culture and gender variables in their research approaches. On the other hand, anthropologists usually do not investigate the role of individual differences when studying community processes and therefore cannot conceptualize those differences. Only by combining both perspectives can we have a sufficiently comprehensive framework to understand and influence how to create prosocial communities.

Both Alan and Beth have complex social and cultural backgrounds, yet both are planning to use similar empirically tested knowledge and techniques when teaching. Alan went to a parochial grade school so is comfortable with some religious rituals in the classroom. Beth went to a selective private school that provided many extracurricular and cultural experiences but included religious activities only in relation to a few holidays. Alan's religious experiences and teaching emphasized moral strictures and fixed rituals but little active participation in religious services and a clergy who mediated God-related concerns. Beth's religious experiences emphasized active expression of emotions as part of church services and direct responsibility for her own conscience and mediation with her God. Thus, Alan's and Beth's nested religious frameworks provide them with distinctly different expectations of others outside of their religious communities. This nested framework information gives us an understanding of how they, their students, and the school will affect and be affected by their participation.

In sum, we human beings create all of our systems of explanation; thus, they have a subjective nature which is derived from our distinctive personal equations. The chief difference between our personal explanation systems lies in which beliefs we take for granted and which are believed open to inquiry and investigation. As suggested in the preceding section about ethnic validity, the interrelationships between our unquestioned and our empirically-based understandings are an integral and often overlooked part of each of the societal groupings that we use to organize our individual lives, relationships, communities, and societies.

2.2. Prosocial Community Model

The second major facet of this general, interlocking framework is the *Prosocial Community Model* (PCM). People who define themselves as change agents and wish to understand and change communities must realize they cannot do that job on their own. Individual members are the ones who change their communities at all levels by using their active agent capabilities. Outside agents are able to facilitate change only when they work closely with the people involved. There can be no change either in people's individual natures or their communities without at least their passive participation. This model differs from community based participatory approaches only in that it includes expert and self-identified change agents as part of the participatory community.

Even with all of these needed elements available, we also must know what makes a community prosocial before we can begin to create one. We and the people in a community need to know how to participate in it both as individual residents and as people with particular skills and roles in order to make particular kinds of changes. Finally, if change agents are to successfully create prosocial communities, all of those elements must be integrated. That is, we, as agents, have to understand ourselves, our contexts, and how communities function and change.

An appropriate model for establishing a prosocial community must specify the criteria that any community needs to meet before it can be considered prosocial. It must also provide guidance as to what kinds of processes are involved in forming and maintaining such a community. Important social concerns that people struggle with in this process include how to define the nature of their community and how their lives and their communities influence each other. That is, what may be considered fair or just for a person at an individual level may have adverse consequences for their communities, for outsiders who interact with their communities, and/or for themselves as community members. For example, a landlord after giving proper notice may have the legal right to evict a family that has suffered from tragedy and cannot pay the rent. Doing so has devastating consequences for those residents and may be destructive of their neighbors' sense of community. It may also make them angry at the landlord and less willing to respect the landlord's property as well as that of other landlords.

A prosocial community is one in which everyone is concerned with the other members of the community along with the well-being of the community as a whole and with themselves. It includes a prosocial conception of justice for all individual members and the community. Each person is also accorded a sense of dignity; no one is entirely excluded nor is anyone allowed to dominate. Prosocial communities assist people in developing and internalizing a prosocial sense of conscience. They facilitate and sustain the internalizing of a moral sense of judgment that values the well-being of all and the community at large, and considers them to be interrelated. They are also oriented to supporting the continued development of everyone's psychosocial competence. The characteristics of prosocial communities and the individuals in them are similar because they are organically and functionally integrated.

2.2.1. Functional Interaction

Creating and/or sustaining a prosocial community requires that we develop patterns of individual and social interactions that form and serve the overall purposes of prosocial communities, including respect for people's individuality. However, we do not start with a blank slate. We have already been socialized into nested frameworks and societal structures designed to serve other purposes.

We only need to reconceptualize these ongoing approaches in order to create the prosocial community patterns we seek.

2.2.2. *Patterns of Interaction*

It is not enough that we be socialized with an ethnically valid, psychosocially competent orientation. We must also have an understanding of how to interact with other people and with society's institutional agents and agencies, have the skills to do so effectively, and develop the inclination to do so. Some of the required skill involves knowing how to manage the similarities and differences that are part of all interactions. Even though our interactions inevitably become quite complex, they are characterized by common patterns. My approach is to realize that our perspectives and ways of going about life at times *converge* with those of others, at times they *diverge* from them, and at times they *conflict* with them. This approach provides an overall, tripartite schema for understanding and managing the complexities involved in our many types of interactions.

We often agree with others in our views and approaches and even consider these convergences to be a desirable condition, enabling us to build relationships and work collaboratively to achieve shared objectives. However, in any interactions, we inevitably encounter the limits of our areas of convergence. We must then address our divergence, that is, our differences. While these differences may limit our relationships and possibilities for accomplishing shared goals, they can also be a source of new, constructive alternatives. To some extent, the influence of differences depends on how we address them. One available solution is to incorporate a domain of tolerance and acceptance that enables us to accommodate inevitable differences. This approach also broadens the domain of perspectives that are acceptable and, at least potentially, can serve as a source of new possibilities. Another solution is to engage in conflict over our differences. Doing so may lead to finding a way to accommodate each other or it may narrow our range of constructive interactions and destroy our relationships and even our communities Tyler, F. B., Brome, & Williams, 1991).

Alan's education in a parochial urban grade school and urban public high school led him to experience school environments that were quite different from what Beth experienced. He and Beth are likely to define an ideal high school climate quite differently, including the relative desirability of a hierarchically ordered school and authoritarian teaching approach in contrast to a more benign and supportive climate and openness in teaching.

As we have discussed, Alan and Beth are just getting acquainted. Yet they can potentially find many convergences and ways to deal with their divergences; they can not only become collaborative colleagues but friends as well. As they continue to interact, their divergent ways of interacting can reveal unacceptable values and style differences which may become the source of potentially destructive conflicts. However, such conflicts need not result in their personal destruction nor that of their relationship. They can turn to prosocially oriented conflict management approaches that enable them to acknowledge their differences and respect each other's integrity. This limit is, of necessity, one that must be accepted by those involved in any prosocial relationship or prosocial community.

An overall pattern of convergence, divergence, and conflict management provides a cardinal set of guidelines for bridging the gap between maintenance of individual interests and emphasizing a prosocial community orientation. Those guidelines are also essential to follow in the development and maintenance of a prosocial community. That does not mean that relationships between couples or among other social groupings can never be dissolved. It only means that emphasis needs to be placed on managing conflict in ways that retain the integrity of the community as well as the people in it.

2.2.3. Resource Collaboration/Resource Enhancement

A prosocial orientation to interactions will not guarantee a prosocial outcome. Rather, ways of interacting differ in their nature and consequences. In the U.S., the concepts of justice are focused on the establishment of equity between differing parties, particularly in response to an identified injustice (Tyler, T. R., et al., 1997). They do not provide an outcome that will render the injured party better off than before the harmful injustice occurred, nor do they address whether or how the offender and/or the community are improved by the justice process or the outcome. Theories of retributive justice seem to endorse the principle that it is appropriate to punish an offender to such an extent that balance between the parties is restored. That approach may have that effect and may deter others from committing injustices (as is argued in its defense at times), but it all too often does not. Also, there is no implication that it improves any of the individuals involved or their community or in any way renders either more prosocial. One extreme example of retributive justice is the death penalty. This solution does not restore a balance because that is impossible, but injured parties, possibly the family of a murder victim, may gain a sense of revenge or justice. However, killing the perpetrator does not make either him/her or the victim's family become better people. Also, there is not any compelling evidence that it will create a more prosocial society or even, in the long run, help the avenged people feel better or more able to go on with their lives. The only certain outcome is that it will prevent the perpetrator from killing others.

Equity-based exchange relationships such as when a person works for a monetary payment may serve as a universalistic model of justice when extrinsic rewards are involved. That is, in these kinds of exchanges the rewards are not inherently part of the interactions. They only serve to maintain the status quo. They do not enhance prosocial community relationships. Personal relationships such as friendships or other community-oriented groupings are of an intrinsic nature. In them, the values of exchanges are built into the interactions themselves (Deci, 1975). Further, the nature of the interactions is such that all of the parties will potentially benefit from them. When a couple spends time together or friends gather for an outing or a party, it is expected, and often the case, that all involved feel gratified. They complete the activity with a sense of enhanced relationships and well-being. On the other hand, if Alan's or Beth's students say to them, "you don't really care about us; you're just here to use us and move on", they would be suggesting that Alan and Beth are not even offering a very good equity relationship. The students would also be implying that they are starved for some kind of resource enhancing relationship, i.e., "we want somebody to care about us."

What, then, are alternative approaches to relationships that might support and encourage constructive, prosocial interactions rather than just maintain or restore the status quo? The basic idea of resource exchange theory is that people exchange their psychosocial resources (Foa, Converse, Tornblom, & Foa, 1993). Alan and Beth may establish a resource exchange relationship if they decide to share their different background-based understandings of how their students are viewing their lives, their school experiences, and their expectations of teachers. Some resource exchanges may involve multiple interactions within a group of people. Others are particularistic interchanges that are dependent for their meaning on a specific person or persons such as friends or a relationship partner. These exchanges may include companionship or collaborative activities ranging from dancing to preparing a meal to making a quilt or a life or a community together. These activities are resource *enhancing* for all concerned.

The ideas of resource exchange and enhancement seem difficult to use in working with people who have grievously harmed or have murdered others. Even so, involving a harm-doer in some productive activity can begin to return to the victims and the perpetrator even a minimal extrinsic value such as helping to contribute some lost income to dependent members of the victim's family. There is the even further possibility of seeking ways for the two parties to engage in some common activity to prevent other such occurrences. For example, Ryan, (1997) reported on a situation in which a violent youth killed a prosperous man's son while he was working as a pizza delivery man. The murdered son's father sought out the youthful killer; instead, he found the grandfather who had tried to raise his grandson to live within society's rules. The two of them formed a partnership, the *Tarik Khamisa Foundation*, to develop programs for such alienated urban youth. That did not restore the dead son nor get the youthful killer out of jail, but it was a constructive beginning toward creating a more prosocial community by working to give young people some hope and some socially productive skills.

My colleagues and I refer to resource collaboration as a model of how interactions are likely to become resource enhancing (Tyler, F. B., Pargament, & Gatz, 1983; Tyler, F. B., 2001). Relationships can be built on the assumption that human resources are always limited and that everyone has strengths and limitations, i.e., has resources and needs. As we demonstrated in a high school counseling project, everyone gains by working together so that they can exchange their resources with others who need them and themselves receive needed resources in turn. This form of interaction is mutually enhancing. It also introduces collaboration to the participants so they begin to view how their relationships and communities can function prosocially. That is, working together by exchanging resources introduces the model of a prosocial community. My broader assertion is that such an approach to all forms of interactions within society can generally be formulated in this way.

2.2.4. Levels of Action

Berger and Berger (1985) presented the *Levels of Action* framework for the limited task of developing community organization approaches to prevent delinquency. I elaborated on this model to guide the incorporation of such youth into their own communities as full participants (Tyler, F. B., 1997). My goal here is to expand it even further as a central feature of a prosocial community model for guiding the development of all of our communities and societies. The three facets, their ingredients, and their interrelationships are outlined in the following sections.

Locality development. Locality development approaches look for *convergences* among the people or groups within a community. These convergences are then used to identify a shared basis for those people or groups to work together on the issues that concern them. Such an approach is crucial for incorporating marginalized individuals or groups as full, constructive members of a community. Traditionally, marginalized people are devalued as unworthy, antisocial, a drain on a community's resources, and a threat to the well-being of others and the community. Categorized that way, they are then excluded from opportunities to participate in the community; consequently, they can not build on their resources and resourcefulness in order to contribute in meaningful ways, including through employment. The community lost the resources that these individuals could have contributed, and they lost the benefits they could have enjoyed.

Excluded people often face the undesirable options of accepting their reduced status and quality of life or of defining themselves in opposition to the community. In the first instance, they have poorer quality lives, and they and their community are deprived of their potential contribution. In the second instance, they and the rest of the community interact in a destructive conflict style to everyone's detriment. The contrasting position is that before you can incorporate excluded people into a prosocial community, everyone else must first reconceptualize them as being worthy, resourceful, and community resources. From this perspective, Alan and Beth can treat their students as valuable resources in the school and show them how to see themselves in that way. Over time, the school, the broader community, and the students themselves all need to shift to that perspective in their shared views of each other. They need to treat each other as valuable resources so that they all can have the best opportunity to gain from their education and their teaching experiences.

Social planning. Social planning introduces the need for expertise and the role of experts, often professionals, into the community development process. Their role is to improve the community's efficacy and the well-being of everyone, including themselves. Experts bring specialized skills to help solve specific, existing community problems such as youth violence, unemployment, and public health dangers. However, when professionals see themselves as self-contained experts who are not part of the community, they may set up an adversarial relationship with the community and its members rather than a prosocial one. As teachers, Alan and Beth have become part of their classrooms' and the school's social planning enterprise. They can use their expertise to change their students from being alienated to becoming prosocially constructive and also contribute to the community development process of the school. First, however, they have to define themselves as part of that school community to be effective.

Social Action. Social action activities are those leadership and policy directives and programs undertaken by its formal and informal civic leaders to guide the direction of a community. If social action activities are designed to engage segments of the community in non-collaborative conflict with each other, they become agents of destructive change. For example, organizing the privileged members of a community to exclude marginalized citizens' efforts to obtain housing (a not-in-my-backyard approach) is likely to increase class conflict and result in a loss of quality of life for the entire community. If social action activities are directed at creating a more cohesive city that enriches the quality of life of its residents, they are acting to create a prosocial spiral of development. Within the small communities of their classrooms, Alan and Beth become the civic leaders or cultural definers who shape community policies. They may choose to see themselves as separate from the students and maybe even above them, more knowledgeable than the students about what is in their best interest, and, overall, as better people than the students. If they do, the students will conclude that their negative assumptions about Alan's and Beth's motives for teaching in their high school are correct. In that case, Alan's and Beth's efforts are likely to set up struggles in the classroom and defeat the students as learners and their goals as teachers. They will also defeat themselves as individuals. However, Alan and Beth can choose to see the students as like them in having resources as well as needs, and treat them that way. If they use this approach to the students and their classes, they can potentially create a constructive spiral of prosocial development to the benefit of the students and themselves.

Often the culture-defining members (CDGs) of a community see themselves as above or separate from the rest. However, a social action approach requires that the leading individuals and groups in the community come to a realization that their well-being and that of the community and its members are interrelated. Everyone will be better served by acknowledging that they all have both resources and needs. Those needs can be better met by pooling everyone's resources. The culture-defining people need to become full and equal members and participants in the community just as the non culture-defining people do. Social action approaches to accomplish the development of prosocial communities require that community leaders, who have major responsibilities for establishing rules and policies, facilitate prosocial approaches to problems and mediate conflicting interests and destructive orientations. They can use their influence most effectively when they acknowledge their own interests and involvement and assume a collaborative stance. That approach can reduce destructive conflict and facilitate the building of a more cohesive, prosocially oriented community. Olweus (1991, 1992) found that a coordinated approach which included the community, the schools and teachers, the parents, and the children themselves led to the reduction of bullying in Norwegian schools. In that situation, participation of the community leadership was vital to the development of effective social change programs.

When CDGs assume an elitist, detached, or condescending role, they contribute to the non-collaborative conflicts all too evident in communities which are segregated by status and economic barriers or by physical barriers such as gated housing. Alan and Beth are not yet in a position to be considered leaders who can change the school's policies and climate, but they can change their classrooms by their actions; they can set an example not only for their own students but also for others in the school. Eventually, they can build on the approaches that they learn from their current teaching experiences to influence their own communities through their work and their contributions as citizens.

2.3. Integration of the Ethnic Validity and Prosocial Community Perspectives

It is important to understand that the term, *transcultural*, in the TEV model is used in two ways. Primarily, it describes the shared framework that provides for a common understanding among a community of people about what constitutes an appropriate way to conduct their shared existence. It also refers to the unique transcultural framework that each of us has and is valid for each of us. That is, each of us is a community of one. To form prosocial communities of two or more, we must each enlarge our own ethnic validity configurations to extend beyond ourselves and include the legitimacy of the ethnic validity of others around us. These broader configurations encompass the diversity of the multiple perspectives held by people in any group. They are also the basic level at which people begin to interact, whether they are from the same family or from two distinct cultural groups. We all must assume the task of developing this broadened sense that others are legitimate in their own ways if we are to establish more encompassing *transcultural* communities.

Creating a widely accepted TEVM out of more limited ones is a necessary step in any effort to develop, maintain, or even understand prosocial communities. Specifically, having that as a goal provides the necessary focus for people to identify and work out patterns of communication and interaction, including conflict resolution and community development. That goal also highlights the importance of being sensitive to and accommodating of differences when efforts are made to establish prosocial patterns of interaction and prosocial communities.

We live in societies that are made up of communities. If these communities are prosocial ones that accord all members dignity, none is completely dominant, and none is entirely excluded, they become optimal forms of society. Such societies can be developed and maintained only by the voluntary, discretionary participation of their members and their internested communities. When people internalize these characteristics, it becomes natural for them to function together to inform and improve their communities in prosocial ways.

Societies are large, heterogeneous groupings, and made up of complex and often contradictory patterns of interaction among their people. To influence interactions in a manner that brings communities together in a prosocial way requires coordinated efforts. The more both CDG and NCDG fellow residents become willing participants in the community because they are valued and respected members, the more they become prosocial community oriented. Further, as people cooperate they find out directly how much their well-being is improved when they form resource enhancement patterns and use them to guide themselves and their broader societies.

3 The Current Situation: Psychologists' Approaches to Community Change

I have based the Transcultural Ethnic Validity Model (TEVM), the framework described in the previous chapters, on the findings from fifty years of work by behavioral and social scientists, including myself, to understand human well-being and dysfunction. The framework is based on the outcomes of these efforts to understand and sustain social and psychological change in individuals and societies. The goals of these efforts have ranged from enhancing the capabilities of people and/or organizations to reducing their vulnerabilities or correcting their destructive characteristics. Some of them were directed toward changing individuals, others toward changing the ways in which societies are organized and function, and still others toward changing the complex interactions in and among community systems. An examination of this history shows us how this work has led to the approaches currently used by community psychologists. This history can help us understand the strengths and limitations of various approaches and also gives clear indications as to why we need a prosocial community oriented perspective for long term, effective results in our community development work. The examples I have included are significant in indicating, at times by what they omitted, the importance of building prosocial communities and steps toward that goal.

3.1. Background

Personally, I received my professional education before there was an area of community psychology. The community mental health and community psychology movements in the post World War II climate of the United States arose from the realization that the available individually oriented clinical approaches to restore the health of psychologically dysfunctional veterans would never be adequate. The country was also struggling with the pressures of burgeoning societal responsibilities to provide civil rights for all and whether to return to a more individualistic and less socially progressive society. That context of social turmoil led to the development of numerous community approaches.

My entry into the field emerged gradually as the limitations of a clinical perspective became apparent, and I felt a need to give more consideration to the contextual issues in people's lives. As I became more involved in social change, the line between my personal and professional roles began to disappear because they became more intertwined. As I mentioned earlier, while working with a non-governmental program trying to improve the lives of street children in Bogota, Colombia, my wife (a nurse/applied anthropologist) and I were asked to help with research to document the children's view of the world in order to counter the professionally based world-views that were being imposed on them. We found that many of those youths had prosocial concerns for each other and hopes for a productive life in society even though they knew they were struggling against enormous obstacles and a society that was hostile toward them. It seemed imperative to us and the agency with which we were collaborating that in addition to professional publications we need to provide our research findings to their street educators and others in ways that could help these and other marginalized children (Tyler, F. B., Tyler, S. L., Echeverry, & Zea, 1991).

In 1950, Brewster Smith had argued persuasively for using a multi criterion approach to define both wellness and illness and for viewing wellness as an optimal (functionally useful) rather than maximal (more of everything) balance of wellness characteristics. Smith focused on adjustment, integration, and cognitive (including emotional) adequacy as core characteristics of well-being, and established that these attributes are frequently mutually incompatible. Any reality oriented pattern of personality integration will necessarily be somewhat internally and externally contradictory and yield both benefits and costs.

M. Jahoda (1950) had emphasized that Smith's earlier definitions of autonomous functioning and independence reflected a Western, individualistic bias. She was the major proponent of the notion that a hypothetical, optimally integrated adaptation (unified, internally-consistent personality) might not be ideal for everyone. She pointed out that in a complex society, learning to compromise may be the ideal way to adapt to the conflicting demands of its many different parts. Jahoda joined Smith in giving greater emphasis than had their predecessors and contemporaries to the position that wellness can only be defined in relation to cultural and other contextual considerations; that is, it is a psychosocial status more appropriately called well-being. Skill in independent functioning may be an important characteristic of wellness in individualistic societies. Even so, it may hinder a person's ability to participate effectively in the numerous collaborative, dependent, and co-dependent relationships that are vital to family and community functioning. Further, a preference for cooperative, collaborative, and other forms of collective functioning may be a more important component of psychological well-being in more interdependent societies.

The problem with this important insight is that the fields of personality, community psychology, and community mental health are dominated by universalist perspectives which assume that individual personality and human well-being exist independently of external circumstances. This view maintains that individuals will experience psychological well-being if they acquire a set of tools for dealing constructively with their life events regardless of their circumstances. That position overlooks the fact that one criterion of human well-being is a constructive adjustment to the circumstances that communities impose on people. Consistent with this orientation, the individual's impact on the community (unless it is negative) is not included as a criterion of the person's well-being. In other words, whether being independent, dependent, aggressive, passive, competitive, or collaborative will contribute to well-being depends, in part, on the circumstances.

A United States Joint Commission on Mental Illness and Health was established to study the country's mental health issues and recommend public policy directions. One of the task forces, headed by M. Jahoda (1958) and commissioned as part of that effort, was charged with the complex task of defining positive mental health (presumably including psychological wellness). It also tried to differentiate mental health from mental illness and establish the relative influence of individuals and their contexts in determining their behavior. The idea that well-being is more than the absence of mental illness and is dependent on circumstances was the pivotal step in developing a concept of positive mental health as more than the medically based term of wellness. Rather, positive mental health as represented in the contexts of community mental health and community psychology is more accurately defined as a psychosocial state of well-being.

It seems clear that a single, universal definition of positive mental health or other such optimal status is inadequate as a criterion for defining human well-being and maladaptation. Rather, well-being is likely a mosaic of both complementary and contradictory internal and external attributes. It is a balance of positive and negative, subjective and behavioral outcomes. The balance may take the form of a complex integration of both general and situationally specific configurations of attributes rather than a particular cohesiveness of a few, universalist characteristics. Further, well-being is likely to be attainable only if certain minimal external as well as internal conditions are present.

3.2. Community Mental Health/Psychology Approaches

In general, community-oriented approaches to intervention differ from individualistic ones in their view of the relationship between the individual and the community. This section provides an overview of approaches that seek community change by focusing on changing individuals, others on those that modify social systems, and still others that change people and system interactions. Each approach has its distinctive strengths and limitations, although all of them are concerned with the nature of individuals and communities and directed at promoting well-being and preventing deterioration. To establish how and whether an approach contributes to the creation of prosocial communities, I will critique each area separately and start by examining the ones that are directed at changing individuals. The chapter will conclude with a look at how we can begin to reconceptualize how we approach our work with communities.

3.2.1. Changing Individuals

As noted, some community psychology approaches try to improve communities by changing individuals in groups in particular ways without regard to their individual or community circumstances. In these cases, the goal is to aid or enable individuals (usually those who meet designated criteria, e.g., marginal ethnic or economic status) in ways that will lead them to make their own changes in their situation. Other approaches try to enhance the well-being (however defined) of recipients by assisting them to overcome or reduce the debilitating effect of their vulnerabilities or limitations, regardless of their life context. The impact of these types of approaches is limited because they do not consider that people sometimes live in circumstances which permit only a very limited quality of life or sense of well being. As the following examples illustrate, a pathway to well-being often requires major changes in peoples' environments that are beyond the capabilities of the individuals in them.

3.2.1.1. Psychological Well-being

To consider the relationship between communities, prosocial or otherwise, and the well-being (psychological wellness) of the individuals in them, we need to have a working definition of psychological well-being. Unfortunately, I have been unable to find any definition of wellness in the social science literature, including that of psychology. Available information is limited because of several problematic reasons, including that these are somewhat open ended and elusive conditions; however, there is a dictionary definition of well-being (see Chapter One). In United States society, an individual's wellness is defined by health officials in terms of specified thoughts and behaviors chosen from a predetermined list of imprecise characteristics. Some consider wellness to be a completely subjective attribute. This position leaves us with a dilemma. If it is essential to eliminate or protect against negative environmental factors in order to prevent individual psychological breakdown, why are environmental factors considered irrelevant to definitions of individual psychological wellness? Even though people are considered to have some capacity for agency or choice, does that mean that there are no external determinants that influence their behavior? Also, is wellness entirely an individual phenomenon? Can an organization or a community have a sense of wellness? I think rather that the best resolution of this dilemma, at least in the field of community psychology, is to abandon the concept of wellness in favor of well-being as I defined it in Chapter One. To repeat, it means "feeling good about one's self, one's life, one's neighbors and neighborhoods, one's community, and about the world beyond."

A useful reference point from which to consider these questions is *The Handbook of Community Psychology* (Rappaport & Seidman, 1999). Its well-qualified contributors have collected, condensed, and integrated the major developments in their field as of the end of the twentieth century. One of the core issues they attended to was psychological wellness. A discussion by van Uchelen (1999) of individualistic and interdependent (collectivistic) foci provides a useful background for considering how wellness has been addressed. He pointed out that an individualistic orientation has so dominated psychology that we unquestionably accept it as a worldwide shared view of reality. In contrast, members of more collectivist (interdependent or prosocially oriented) societies define their well-being in relation to how they perceive the conditions of others. For example, van Uchelen and colleagues (van Uchelen, Davidson, Quressette, Brasfield, & Demerais, 1997) studied views of "First Canadians" (Native Americans) about their health, wellness, and life strengths. Their respondents focused on the well-being of their families and the health-promoting traditions of their communities rather than on themselves. Based on their reports, they clearly believe that there are at least minimal external criteria that must be met before they consider themselves to be, and are considered to be, psychologically well.

Similarly, Katz (1984) and his colleagues (Katz & Seth, 1987) define and describe synergistic communities as ones in which well-being is enhanced by a collectivist approach. They differentiated between a *scarcity paradigm* and a *synergy paradigm*. In a synergy paradigm, human resources are considered to be renewable and expanding, unlike in a scarcity paradigm in which they are considered limited. That is, people's positive activities such as helping and healing can be increased by sharing resources with each other. Sharing communities become highly cohesive and, among other characteristics, members willingly contribute psychological resources to each other. Members create a synergism through their connections to the community which provides a collective psychological energy. That synergism enables people to participate in the community and build relationships with each other through activities that enrich them as well as the community.

van Uchelen and Katz and their colleagues do not differentiate individual from system change as they see the two as inextricably interrelated. However, they are mentioned here to illustrate the psychosocial nature of well-being. In contrast, psychologists' present conceptions of community and psychological wellness tend to be based on a *scarcity* paradigm with its focus of separating people's individual and social concerns. Their paradigmatic assumption is that resources are limited. Thus, individual resources must be shepherded since, for example, if it is assumed that there is a limited supply of love, then if an individual loves one person s/he has less to give to others. From this viewpoint, individuals must compete for scarce community resources, as in the "commons" example (see Chapter One) or as with water in the desert. Individuals' relationships and relational characteristics must also be shepherded. In this type of paradigm, the concept of empowerment (discussed in detail in later sections) and its implication of force seem more germane than that of enablement with its presumption of sharing, reciprocity, and mutual benefit.

The current dominance of individualistic scarcity paradigm orientations in community as well as in mainstream psychology has led us to largely ignore or reject the need and even possibility of asking whether social conditions contribute to or constrain psychological wellness or dysfunction. The result is that we have few community or community process concepts of wellness and little research about them. For example, Cowen focused on "routes to wellness" rather than wellness per se. To him, wellness differs under different circumstances and becomes more complex with aging. It has "significant person-related (both dispositional and experiential), transactional, and environmental determinants" (Cowen, 1999, p. 83). He defined wellness more specifically by citing as exemplars competence, empowerment, and resilience. Each of these characteristics has been advanced separately as the major factor underpinning wellness. Cowen assigned a foundational role to competence. Specifically, one value of competence is that "by eliciting personal satisfaction, [it] helps the person to form an image of self as effective and worthwhile" (p. 87). He also saw competence as a significant factor contributing to resiliency. That is, a level of competence enables us to rebound from frustrations and attain goals and objectives. We have a reason to feel good about ourselves and be effective at bouncing back after setbacks.

While Cowen's (1999) work added some useful characteristics to our understanding of wellness, we are again left with questions about its relevance to prosocial communities. For example, he noted that empowerment involves motivation and skill (competence), but he did not define the requirements of a *masterable* environment. Unless a situation can be brought under control or a problem solved, no one can become empowered. Rappaport (1981) considered empowerment as the gateway to "a more equitable, fair, and just society" (p. 88). However, it is not clear how empowerment with its individualistic and power oriented emphasis can help develop a prosocial community orientation.

Cowen (1999) argued that a psychological wellness framework is a better umbrella than primary prevention for developing community programs and promoting wellness. He said that we need much more research to formulate an umbrella view, apparently assuming that gaining knowledge would help us resolve conflicts between individualistic and prosocial views. Although he wrote about problems of individual injustice or deprivation, he did not address the destructive individual and social effects of institutionalized characteristics such as racism, authoritarianism, or a highly individualistic society. Finally, Cowen did not discuss the importance of creating a prosocial orientation with its sense of duty and synergy as elements essential to the formulation of a broad based approach to psychological wellness.

The marginalized children in Hawaii whom Emma Werner followed throughout their childhood development and into adulthood are examples that show us how psychosocial support and resilience contribute to well-being. These youth, in spite of severe stressors, "worked well, played well, loved well and expected well" (Werner, 1989, p. 28). Werner also stressed that these children had at least one important caring and supportive person during their lives. That is, resilience is relevant to attaining and retaining a sense of well-being, but its development is somewhat contingent on environmental circumstances, in this case on the presence of a supportive adult.

A wellness orientation is too limited to be a central organizing principle as a community development model. From my perspective, what Cowen has called wellness is better thought of as well-being and defined as a dynamic state of living. In that sense, well-being is like maintaining balance on a bicycle. It involves having the skills and sense of mastery required to invite and address life's opportunities and challenges with confidence. That balance-based sense of well-being means having confidence that life's events can not only be survived, but prevailed over in a manner that yields satisfaction and interest in facing future events with pleasant anticipation. Of course, as with riding a bicycle, when the road or overall environment becomes unmanageable, balance cannot be achieved and all that can be done is to survive, if possible, until circumstances change. Unlike on a bicycle trip taken by oneself, we live in social contexts. Nesting our definition of wellness and our approach to it in a prosocially oriented psychosocial framework gives us a way to combine each person's commitments to his/her own well-being with those of the collaborative and synergistic strengths of a prosocial community orientation.

This kind of formulation seems much more appropriate than a context-free formulation for enabling us to understand, for instance, Alan and Beth as they emerge from college and enter their adult careers. That is, wellness is often defined as independent of relationships to the outside world. In actuality, individual and community well-being are intertwined or interdependent. For example, it would be difficult to argue that Alan and Beth have identical senses of what well-being means to them. Their senses of themselves and their worlds have been constructed in quite different contexts although they both seem to have a sense of mastery acquired in their respective environments. Also, as they begin their first full entry into adult roles it seems unlikely that their respective senses of well-being can be sustained independently of their relationship to or effectiveness in their new environment.

3.2.1.2. Pathology and Disorder Prevention

The historical and current mainstream approaches to mental illness and health in the United States and other Western oriented countries are characterized by a broad-based medical, epistemological, and community mental health model of pathology prevention. Felner, Felner, and Silverman (1999) described the historical, blended public health model which encompasses a full range of traditional medical and human-service interventions including tertiary (preventing further deterioration in established cases), secondary (early intervention after onset of symptoms), and primary (intervention with at risk individuals to prevent onset of symptoms) prevention. They proposed replacing the public health approach with a unique prevention model restricted to primary prevention. They asserted that secondary and tertiary prevention are not prevention, they are treatment. They redefined secondary prevention as early intervention, and tertiary prevention as treatment. From this perspective, primary prevention is the only before-the-fact intervention. However, consistent with the public health model, it is not directed at individuals, but at population groups or demographic segments of a population shown to exhibit more destructive characteristics and/or fewer positive ones. For example, enriched preschool programs and early sex education programs are considered systematic efforts to facilitate processes that lead to improved adaptation and increased well-being. Such programs also may protect against and decrease the occurrence of disorders.

Felner, et al.'s (1999) shift from pathology-oriented, descriptive terms to disorder-oriented ones established a different paradigmatic conception. It emphasized that peoples' thoughts, feelings, and behaviors of concern are primarily psychosocial in character; that is, they need to be understood as disorders of functioning that are not entirely a function of internal biomedical states. Rather, they are indications of disordered internal and external psychosocial states which are in part reflections of disordered personal and social histories. This shift in structural and functional orientation also turned the field's focus toward primary prevention and away from secondary and tertiary intervention efforts. That is, it refocused the field's efforts toward prevention of potential dysfunction.

When causes of mental disorders are seen to be psychological factors, prevention can be redefined as intentional, before-the-fact actions directed at disruption of the path to disorder for entire populations. Prevention can also now include activities to facilitate the path to well-being for populations. Interventions might switch from empowering the population to that of changing their social circumstances. A criterion of the effectiveness of these efforts would be, for example, a reduction in the number of cases of dysfunction identified in a population following an intervention. Another relevant criterion, although one that has been less emphasized, would be an increase in the number of those reporting higher levels of resilience in dealing with inevitable difficulties.

A primary prevention approach requires that the path to positive outcomes can be known and be influenced; otherwise intervention is impossible. One such model, advanced by Sameroff and Fiese (1989), is called a *transitional-ecological* model of development. It stresses that the development of people's psychosocial characteristics is a product of their bidirectional interactions between themselves and their contexts. These interactions are assumed to be influenced not just by the proximal ecology but by each person's entire life contexts, from the very individual and intimate to the broadest ecological and cultural facet, e.g., marriage and divorce-related changes in living conditions, family celebrations and tragedies, economic prosperity and depression, etc. In other words, their argument is that the path to positive outcomes involves all of these factors, and they must be taken into consideration in treatment approaches.

Overall, primary prevention approaches involve systematic actions and are founded on the belief that people can learn and change. They build on the assumption that the most important way to reduce the occurrence of dysfunctional behavior is to intervene at a population (school, community, etc.) level. Their aim is to increase supportive and constructive behaviors and teach prosocial skills while also eliminating destructive influences in people's lives.

Felner et al., (1999) wrote that intervention activities should lead to multiple outcomes because many of the contributors to disorder have been found to be interrelated, developmentally complex, and non-linear in nature. They formulated and described an empirically based approach to integrating a psychosocial perspective with a life span perspective. They pointed out that societies and communities vary in their values and approaches, and therefore, they also have different strengths and problems. Even so, Felner and his colleagues argued that an approach that promotes strengths (e.g., resilience) and reduces negative factors (e.g., depression) can be productively undertaken without trying first to define the general character of prosocial or dysfunctional communities and their residents. They also suggested that the kinds of changes they envision can be more effectively introduced as components of comprehensive social change efforts.

In the final analysis, both Felner et al., (1999) and Cowen (1999) obscured the difference between the prevention of dysfunction and the promotion of well-being when they argued for a combined prevention and social intervention approach. As in the well-being orientation described earlier, their efforts are directed at populations, not communities or societies. Even so, their goals, processes, and proposed improvements have a generally specifiable character and offer many potential advantages over a more limited biomedical approach. However, unless their social intervention activities include a prosocial community enrichment orientation they cannot fully extend their activities beyond a pathology prevention focus. They provide no way to include the potential benefits of synergistic spirals of individual and collaborative development. Consequently, their framework cannot effectively include psychosocially based synergistic and other growth and maturational possibilities.

As an alternative to the prevention focus of avoiding negative outcomes, an *education model* might be more appropriate. An education model is based on the belief that the most effective intervention strategy is to teach people to induce and enhance protective factors at a population level. For example, economically impoverished communities have poor schools, environmental stressors, and few models of high expectations. The solution is to "provide to all children and families strong preschool programs, high-quality educational environments, safe neighborhoods, the removal of policies that create disincentives for family success, and access to quality employment opportunities" (Felner, et al., 1999, p. 20). Or, if the goal is to reduce the divorce rate, then followers of an educational perspective undertake changes that will provide adequate child care for all parents in order to reduce their stress levels.

Thus, the education model provides a different perspective on the nature of the complex processes of living and restricts consideration of biomedical factors to a role of limiting or strengthening the capability level of people in the population, e.g., removing lead from environments. This approach contrasts with the traditional one of, for example, waiting until after the divorce and then doing further testing of the children to establish whether their stress levels have increased. From the educational perspective, priority is assigned to formulating an intervention model that will increase identifiable strengths in order to increase the quality of life and social contributions of those involved, not primarily or exclusively to prevent or reduce the occurrence of specifiable disorders.

The educational system in any society is the sanctioned bureaucratic societal organization designed to prepare succeeding generations to fulfill roles and obligations in order to sustain and lead that society. Further, in the United States, elementary school systems often include informal parents' organizations as well as their formal, publicly defined governing structures. This involvement of parents often enriches the quality of schools and the educational experiences of the children, particularly when they and the managers of the school form a prosocial relationship. However, in spite of this potentially prosocial systems approach, the educational system in the U. S. and other individualistic societies may be limited by its orientation to educating and ranking individual students.

3.2.2. Changing Social Systems

Even though the approaches just discussed have emerged from a community mental health orientation, they are focused on directly changing individuals by altering the external forces that affect them, thereby indirectly changing their community. In contrast, other community oriented approaches directly address the broader forces that are integral parts of communities. The assumption in these undertakings is that individuals are not autonomous agents or, at most, have limited capabilities. Efforts to change individuals are indirect through modification of ecological factors or other kinds of social systems or institutions. For example, these approaches may be employed in efforts to make major changes in the society's educational and social control institutions, scholarly disciplines, and work settings. In one way or another, the primary goal is to change the life contexts within communities for their individual members. However, the areas where these approaches can be used are limited. School or mental health programs often do not address or involve the community government, informal structures, other community organizations, or the citizens generally. The important point is that this category of social change efforts is often not primarily concerned with the community in the sense that it is a group of people living in proximity and with a common sense of identity and relatedness to each other and each other's welfare. Instead, social change efforts are often directed at one, or a part of one, community component.

3.2.2.1. Ecological Approaches

The field of ecology is focused on understanding the relationships between systems' characteristics, the individuals in the system, and the resources (kinds of energy) that are put into the system to develop, sustain, or destroy it. For example, an aquarium is a contained ecology. For the plants and animals in it to survive, a balance must be maintained between the numbers of each living thing, the light, temperature, and other elements entered into that aquarium. Analysis of an ecology assigns no special value to any specific facet of a system, and it provides no basis for intervening. In order to use this approach with people, a community's members must make some individual and collective value assumptions if they are to move beyond that neutral stance, maintain their own survival, and improve the quality of their lives. The impact of these kinds of assumptions and the ways they are implemented are illustrated in the following paragraphs.

Kelly and his colleagues were among the first community oriented psychologists to argue that an ecological approach to social systems could be of value in developing a *community-based* community psychology. To them, "the essence of the ecological perspective is to construct an understanding of the interrelationships of social structures and social processes of the groups, organizations, and communities in which we work" (Kelly, Ryan, Altman, & Stelzner, 1999, p. 133). They use the ecological perspective to outline a model that produces social system change through preventive interventions. Proactive interventions change the interdependencies of the ecology to become more beneficial, that is, oriented to connecting the people with the system in a prosocial manner that develops both personal and social resources.

Kelly et al., (1999) identified the structural and procedural factors crucial to developing and maintaining a positive social system. They worked out a framework that includes the essential personal and social resources and social settings and systems factors needed to develop and maintain positive social systems. They then argued that

> The field of community psychology offers a novel and compelling opportunity to conduct research and create services so that persons in social systems can create their own resources and settings to enhance their quality of life. An ecological perspective is directed to that purpose, and includes an explicit value framework to help clarify how a system can be a resource and not be stultifying. (Kelly, et al., 1999, p. 155)

Kelly, et al's (1999) work provided a holistic and integrative approach applicable to any system's relevant preventive orientation. Their approach has made an important contribution with its emphasis on the interdependence among the individuals, processes, and structures of systems. However, its focus was primarily limited to helping the involved individuals understand how their system can be a resource to them instead of a frustration. The scope of their approach could have been much greater had they paid attention to the community system's relationships and exchanges with interfacing external systems.

Trickett, Barone, and Watts (1999) focused on Mental Health (MH) Consultation as a major, ecologically-oriented community psychology/community mental health approach to systems level preventive interventions. Their assumption is that knowledge of the social context and of the individuals' embeddedness in it are fundamental to understanding and intervening in communities in ways that will enhance their well-being. To describe a community's ongoing functioning, Trickett and his colleagues used four basic ecological principles: *adaptation* (people and other factors keep changing to survive); *cycling of resources* (how can resources be used differently to create change); *interdependence* (people depend on each other and those patterns influence how change will occur); and *succession* (the context and people have evolved in ways that will influence change and future possibilities). Theoretically, these considerations serve as guides to their work.

However, Trickett and his colleagues (1999) highlighted that in reality most MH consultations do not take contextual factors into consideration. Further, the host environment of a consultation is usually not the community, but some organization within it. Even so, consultants have made and can continue to make contributions to system changes that may indirectly benefit or disrupt associated communities and their residents. For example, viewing MH consultation from an ecological perspective orients it toward considering the influence of system changes in an organization on the mental health of the community where it is located. Ecological community factors include indigenous and other resources, diversity, and values relating to the community's mental health.

This research also focused on the individual (Trickett, et al., 1999) It emphasized that the people who make up any setting and function within it are diverse along many dimensions, including gender, ethnicity, socioracial origins, and urban/rural environments. Further, they function within their respective ecologies. A fundamental aspect of an ecological perspective is the idea that people are influenced by their holistic and interactive perspectives. People guide their perceptions and ways of addressing their situations by the characteristics of those contexts. Consultants must be sensitive to the fact that the system or individual markers that are relevant change from context to context. For example, efforts to improve playground facilities in a community may face quite different community dynamics than efforts to reduce drug trafficking.

Further, as Trickett et al., (1999) pointed out, most mental health consultations do not focus on either community development or the role of ecological factors in consultation enterprises. In particular, their approach is limited in not considering what their influence is in ways beyond their identified objectives. It is further limited because it does not address value issues such as whether a consultee organization will be better served by an individualistic justice and scarcity of resources solution or a community oriented, prosocial, synergistic solution.

3.2.2.2. Social Systems Approaches

In the national attempt to create a community approach to mental health in the 1960s, service units called "catchment areas" were established. These units were based on numbers of people in a geographic area. Organizing mental health services in accordance with the boundaries of natural communities was not considered, although catchment areas were to function as "communities". This approach forcibly grouped people together who had no established social relationships and few common concerns. Although the national mandate specified the necessity of citizen involvement in an effort to foster a community approach, guidelines were not provided as to what that meant, nor did the people in these areas have any history of such participation. High priority was assigned to involving mental health professionals. Unfortunately, those professionals were resistant to a community ideology and approach to practice. They were experienced with and favored professional control and a treatment orientation. In addition, the community mental health centers (CMHCs) that were established were organized and managed largely by a technical staff. They, too, were trained in and oriented toward a professional practice approach based on a diagnosis and treatment of disease model. Consequently, services were provided according to status quo practices without consideration of whether they were appropriate to the community's situation and understanding of mental health issues and professional approaches.

It did not work. If community residents wanted short term help with real-life problems, not more abstract and time consuming insight therapies, they had to go elsewhere. Heller and his colleagues (1999) emphasized that the failure of this approach to achieve its main objective was hardly surprising. They also noted

> Suppose the primary mandate of community mental health centers had been the enhancement of psychological and social functioning, rather than the treatment of disability. Most citizens would agree that they should have a say in shaping programs to enhance their own well-being; their active involvement in programs would have increased the likelihood of adoption and adherence. Here we see the power of conceptual models. Because treatment models defined the mental health field, both professionals and citizens alike assumed that the new mental health structures must serve treatment functions. This ideology was "built in" from the start and determined that the new centers would have a treatment, rather than a prevention, focus. (Heller et al., 1999, p. 448)

Predictably, the CMHC pathology-oriented approach failed to deliver on the original vision of a community-based approach for managing the psychosocial well-being of communities and their members. The approach could not address the troubling issues of values, resources, differences in perspectives, and personal involvements that are crucial to the functioning of communities and the people in them. What was required was a new social systems model that provided appropriate roles for the professionals and staff assigned to implement these centers as well as for the community citizens included in their oversight and the people to be served by them. Using a hierarchical professional model of treatment to address the dysfunctions of the community and its members was simply inappropriate because the values and beliefs of the care giver and the client were disjointed from the beginning.

Social systems are organized units that people construct and maintain to serve specified common purposes. In complex societies, such systems are usually formed and sustained by an organized community of professionals; that is, they are discipline-specific such as law or medicine. However, the structure and functioning of any one social system are influenced by many other social systems and disciplines, and by the people that the social system is presumably designed to serve. Historically, the leading disciplines are rooted in established formal and informal ways to manage any given social context and protect their status and influence.

When we look directly at the relationships between social systems and community psychology/community mental health (CMH) systems, the unique aspects of communities and our relationship to them become evident. As described in Chapter Two, everyone is born into a series of progressively more general and abstract systems that function as nested communities. The most basic of these is the family, but also included are our schools, religious institutions, work settings, communities, cultures, and even our species. Communities can be analyzed as social systems and responded to accordingly, but doing so does not completely encompass our relationships to them. For example, at some time in our lives all of us require and rely on physical supports to protect ourselves from natural and human disasters as well as our own frailties. To be entitled to the physical and social supports that we require, we may need to take individual initiatives to sustain our communities by participating in them and assuming some responsibility to sustain them.

A systems approach can be used from an external, detached perspective when intervening in communities. However, that approach cannot serve as a basis for addressing the internal, enmeshed perspectives that are part of how communities function. A community-based strategy requires consideration of the interests of individuals as well as of the structures and processes of the community. Conversely, a systems approach may focus only on considerations that affect those in a community system as a population unit and that system's particular internal and external interests. Acknowledging that these disconnects are built into systems-based strategies is a critical and long ignored source of problems within the fields of community psychology and community mental health.

When beginning to address the task of developing a viable CMH system, Heller, Jenkins, Steffen, and Swindle (1999) focused on the role of disciplines in defining and influencing the evolution and functioning of communities, their institutions, and their settings. They described community psychology as being organized to serve the discipline and its members, not the community. The field has focused largely on providing remunerative professional assistance to specific segments of a population in ways that interest the profession's members while neglecting to serve the community as a whole. For example, community psychologists may consult with an educational system and provide a service to the client schools in that system. The schools may, in turn, help the psychologists by providing research opportunities or even making changes that the consulting psychologists request to benefit their own enrolled children. Such arrangements may benefit both the consultants and the school system; however, they do not focus on involving or improving the entire community. To have a positive impact on communities, it is necessary to become part of them and serve their interests as well as our personal and professional ones.

Heller et al., (1999) elaborated further on this disconnect and the problems it created in developing a community mental health system in the United States. The initial, national efforts to address the country's burgeoning mental health problems were conceptualized as a war against an external enemy. However, "the confrontation of social problems is not the same as 'wars' with external enemies against whom citizens can rally. Social and psychological problems involve entrenched attitudes and practices within the fabric of society, and there are no clear guidelines as to how to proceed" (Heller et al., 1999, p. 448). To address those issues within society, psychologists must work within the fabric of which they are a part. Thus, struggling with social problems is much more like working out issues within one's family.

Other research has also addressed this disjointedness (e.g., Rappaport & Seidman, 1999). A particularly concise and apt summary of this kind of disconnect and what is involved in attempting to overcome it in the United States' public school system has been provided by Weinstein, Gregory, and Strambler (2004). They pointed out that:

> Psychology, in part responsible for the creation of an inequitable culture for learning, must assume leadership in its undoing. It must put in its place a new understanding of the malleable and diverse nature of human capability, the qualities of optimal environments that promote development, and the methods by which social settings can be coherently strengthened to better meet the needs of all children. (p. 18)

Their argument is that we need to create a new and different ecologically-based educational system. That new system must be dedicated to educating everyone in their full diversity. The criteria we use to sort and rank the students as they negotiate that system must be responsive to some of their diverse needs such as levels of academic proficiency. Currently, they do not take into account the nature of the students' ecological backgrounds, differences in kinds of abilities and aspirations, and the variety of ways people learn. All students need to learn basics, i.e., reading, writing, and arithmetic, but to emphasize only one or two areas such as science and mathematics ignores the talents and interests of many students. The current system does not respond to those students' needs in ways that can bring them all in to the society. Confronting that massive disconnection will require not only the involvement of local communities, but comparable collaborative efforts at all levels of United States' society. If we are to confront this challenge constructively, among other activities we will welcome the diversity of experiences and perspectives that people such as Alan an Beth can bring to their new role in the educational system. Unfortunately, as our educational system is currently organized, we are more likely to suppress that aspect of each of them in favor of directly and indirectly influencing them to conform to the common, curriculum focused approach.

3.2.3. Interactions among Systems and People

Among others (as I discussed in detail, Tyler, F. B., 2001), Hunter and Riger (1986) have argued that a community oriented approach to mental health alternatives is needed to incorporate the interactions between the community systems and the people in them as a conceptual focus. That is, we psychologists and related social change oriented professionals need to reconceptualize our understanding of mental health in the context of the community. Similarly, we have to change our conceptions of our roles if we are to better serve the psychosocial well-being of our communities and their residents.

Hunter and Riger (1986) pointed to the long history of sociological analysis of the formation of natural social networks. They noted that sociologists have documented that different kinds of communities exist within legally designated geographic areas. They thought largely in terms of three typologies of communities. *Demographic typologies* are identified by the social characteristics of the residents. Historically, in the United States three central dimensions have functioned to create residential segregation: socioeconomic status, family or life cycle status, and racial/ethnic status. *Land use and housing stock* have served as a second indicator of dynamic changes in the cycling and recycling of the physical form and condition of communities. Finally, *the institutional and organizational nature* of communities is the third typology. These dimensions vary from being formally and hierarchically controlled by officials to being more informally and horizontally controlled with significant citizen and community participation. All of these factors exist in each community and contribute to the way communities function. They all must be taken into consideration to accomplish effective change.

Hunter and Riger (1986) also tell us that, in important ways, communities are socially constructed. That is, they are what people define them to be. Sociologists view community interrelatedness as comprised of three dimensions: "(a) the ecological and sustenance community, (b) the social interactional and institutional community, and (c) the social-psychological and cultural community" (p. 62). Research as of the time of their writing supported that these dimensions are somewhat independent. It cannot be assumed that, for example, changing the social-interactional dimensions will necessarily change the social-psychological ones.

These perspectives provide particularly apt contributions for understanding the relevance of a prosocial community approach. Hunter and Riger's (1986) analysis led them to several conclusions and recommendations for policy formation. First, when trying to design CMH programs, the nature and impact of the following six considerations must be taken into account. Programs need to be developed with sensitivity to the parameters of each context. In this case, one size does not fit all. Second, while community development efforts may, in general, be desirable, they can also have detrimental effects on some of the people in the community and on some otherwise desirable, ongoing community activities. Third, having a cohesive, mutually interdependent community is not everyone's highest value. Further, people living in a specific community may formally or informally belong to and identify more with other communities. Thus, identification with their community of residence is only one value among many that must be taken into consideration. Fourth, people organize their lives in relationship to social groups that transcend their community space. These factors must also be considered when trying to understand a community's needs and how to address them. Fifth, because of all of these factors, the nature of people's lives and their communities are influenced in important ways by external forces beyond their control. One of those external forces is the professionally organized, mental health establishment. The community and its residents may well have good reason to be wary of its intrusion and potential insensitivity to their community's ethos. Sixth, it may well be that the resolution of issues within communities that are in their control are going to be the most responsive to a community approach.

However, even internal issues need to be approached with sensitivity to external factors beyond the community's control.

However, shifting to a community dynamics perspectives has presented serious problems of implementation because participating professionals have known little about communities. They have been prepared only to provide clinical treatment rather than work with entire communities or serve as natural helpers. Specifically, Hunter and Riger's (1986) analysis had found that because "the 'disease' of mental illness was not being eradicated but was becoming more epidemic; 'cures' were not found; and symptomatic treatment, such as chemotherapy, was slowly recognized as the bandage of adaptation not the vaccine of preventive health" (p. 56). From this perspective, community psychology interventions also function largely as symptomatic treatment. They added that these failures grew from an incorrect definition of the problem and that a more appropriate definition of mental disorders and more relevant solutions is needed.

3.3. Reconceptualizing Community Approaches

Understanding and working with an approach that incorporates an understanding of community dynamics requires addressing the role of mental health professionals. They are not only contributing professionals, but they also live and work within communities. They are part of those dynamics and need to address how they should present themselves as members and as outsiders. That issue is addressed, though briefly, in the following paragraphs.

Berkowitz (1999) emphasized that community psychologists have primarily focused on large institutions. Consequently, although they have the ability to play many roles, community psychologists have often been remote from the daily life of people and subject to the vagaries of institutional and public support. Berkowitz assumed the often overlooked role of citizen/professional in his own community. In that capacity, he received no pay, no plaudits as a community psychologist, and no professional recognition. He turned away from those concerns and emphasized that "what will remain are family, neighborhood, and home community. They won't go away" (p. 767). Thus, he chose to use his skills as a participant in the process of changing his own community so that it became a better place for its residents, including him and his family.

Berkowitz underscored his belief that, in the future, citizens will have to improve their skills and effectiveness at influencing institutional power and developing local support. Consequently, community psychologists should not only be encouraging people to develop these skills, but should also engage themselves in that activist process. Because of those contributions, Wolff (1999) identified Berkowitz, among others, as *pioneers* of applied community psychology. One of his themes was that these pioneers were not called community psychologists and no specific academic degree was required for their jobs. Wolff saw the failure to include these personal, professionally based activities as a hindrance to the growth of the field of applied community psychology. He recommended that the field's mainstream return to its original focus on social change and include these individuals and their activities as an integral part of it.

Another of those pioneers, Morgan (1999), was director of the primary prevention program at a community mental health center. To Morgan, an integral part of their work was the inclusion of himself and the staff as participants within their own agency community. Thus, he argued, as I did at Swampscott (Bennett, et al., 1966), that the field needs to redefine itself and its membership as being citizen-professionals, professionals-citizens, or participant conceptualizers.

Another pioneer, Chavis (1999), argued from his 25 year history of working in community development activities, that it is a particularly appropriate area in which to implement the common "values of empowerment, prevention, cultural relativism, ecological orientation, social change, and a distaste for victim-blaming" (p. 767). His own attempts to do so involved two interrelated challenges. One was to redefine and extend his role beyond that of professional in order to become actively engaged as a participant in social change efforts. The other challenge was to convince his community psychologist colleagues that he did not need to abandon his identity as a community psychologist just because he was engaged within communities. He concluded by raising and answering two hypothetical questions.

> Can we say that we value prevention, social change, social justice, equality, and equity without taking action and its associated risks? I think not. . . .therefore the best training ground for us, community psychologists, to learn organizing is in our own communities and work places. After all, how can we hope to facilitate the empowerment of others, if we cannot empower ourselves? (Chavis, 1999, p. 771)

Some of the approaches that were examined in this chapter were designed to focus on aspects of the structures of communities. Others were concerned with programs within and outside of communities which impact on their structures and the lives of people in them. None assume that a fully community-oriented approach must address all of these issues in relation to each other because they are interacting aspects of communities. These approaches do not address the community as an ongoing, organized whole, and their advocates do not consider themselves to be willing or unwilling parts of the communities where they work. Even so, they do influence the community, and the people with whom they are interacting may see them as part of the community. A comprehensive community approach attempts to include all of these considerations. The thrust of my argument has been that understanding and providing for the individual and societal well-being of people and their communities requires a model that will incorporate these elements in relation to each other rather than separately. The model that does so is a Prosocial Community Model as nested within a Transcultural Ethnic Validity Model.

4 The Prosocial Effect of Changing One Aspect of a Community

When medicine began the community mental health and overlapping community psychology movements it shifted the mental health framework from one of treating diagnosable illnesses in individuals to one of preventing the occurrence of those kinds of problems. This new objective was to be accomplished by changing at a population level the factors that predisposed people to mental illnesses and/or introducing activities to improve the psychological well-being of the population. This social action policy change introduced unique responsibilities into the social planning activities of mental health personnel. That is, it legitimized their authority to influence particular individuals and their life contexts even though the people were neither diagnosibly ill nor had they or their community been convicted of violating any laws.

This chapter reviews and evaluates representative examples of the various psychologically based efforts to create community change-oriented approaches at one of the three interrelated levels of society that we have been discussing. Those levels concern, respectively: (1) *social actions*, i.e., community policies developed and maintained by civic leaders, (2) *social planning*, i.e., activities of professionals and managers to implement policies on behalf of the community and its members, and (3) *locality development*, i.e., activities by individuals and community members to improve their lives and the community contexts where they live. The focus throughout is on the strengths and limitations of the programs that focus on change at only one of these levels, and on their contribution to the creation of prosocial communities.

4.1. Changing Individuals to Solve Community Problems

The concept of empowerment as a way to change individuals was introduced by Rappaport (1981). It has generally been defined as a process by which people are enabled to gain control over their lives through their own efforts. People are enabled when they are provided with skills, a sense of worth and control of their destiny, a sense of the sociopolitical environment, and access to participation to obtain resources and goals. Thus, an empowerment approach can go beyond a solitary orientation to a collaborative one by including joint efforts to acquire resources, build competence, and even create social change. However, people individually or collectively become empowered only when they make the psychosocial leap to take action.

Empowerment programs have certain characteristics in common, yet they vary in focus and scope. Many are designed to help particular, designated individuals act autonomously or in concert with others to improve their situations. The idea is that changing individuals within their situations can lead to changing the entire society. Empowerment programs vary in their organization and their relationship to individuals and groups outside of the area of concern, including the broader societies in which they are undertaken.

Zimmerman (1999) emphasized that the process for a person to become psychologically empowered is essentially parallel with that of a psychologist learning to empower others. Professionals must redefine themselves as resourceful participants and collaborators who work bidirectionally with people, all of whom are also knowledgeable and resourceful. Community people must redefine themselves as knowledgeable and resourceful participants and collaborators instead of as inadequate and needy. In order to work together and accomplish their objectives, both parties have to acquire and share information about themselves, each other, the community, and how each functions.

The dynamics of these transactions will be different in each undertaking and context. No one can effectively help others become empowered if they define themselves as experts who are helping in some unidirectional way. Learning how to function and acquire the needed analytic, collaborative, and integrative skills can be accomplished only if the psychologist or other change agent becomes a participant in the community's activities. No one can illustrate, model, or teach these concepts and skills to people in a community without having acquired those concepts and skills themselves in previous community settings or by learning them on the job. Conducting a program to help others empower themselves requires working in a shared, empowering way to design, implement, evaluate, and establish that project as a self-sustaining enterprise. Projects to empower others cannot be authored and owned by a community psychologist or other expert because they are never formed that way. Rather, empowerment projects that are conceived and implemented as externally driven are, by nature, counterproductive.

A particularly powerful illustration of the difference between an empowerment approach and a professional service approach is found in health care. Katz and Seth (1987) relied on health-related case studies for providing a well-illustrated account of the issues involved and the consequences of using these different approaches. Specifically, Western professional medicine's approach to healing has first required that a professional designate individuals as needing help because they have identified illnesses. It assumes that ill people are powerless and in need of expert intervention to manage and, if possible, eliminate the illness. Also, modern Western medicine rests on the assumption that there is a limited supply of healing resources that must be utilized as efficiently as possible (*scarcity paradigm*).

The contrasting empowerment approach assumes that the ill person is an active, resourceful individual with unique knowledge about and capabilities for participating in the healing and can also benefit from assistance. That approach includes the idea that everyone involved has something to contribute as well as something to learn. It is based on another assumption, i.e., that some aspects of healing may be limited, but there are other aspects that can be enhanced by including everyone's contributions. For example, the participants in a women's health collective may share their caring for one another and their knowledge from their own experiences. Included may be information about how to manage treatment of a sexually transmitted disease and how to protect their well-being and that of sexual partners. These aspects of the healing are not limited, but may expand and increase as they are shared. They are illustrative of a *synergistic paradigm*.

Katz and Seth summarize, "synergy is never totally absent in a community if that community is to continue. But Western health care systems are characterized by a relative absence of synergy, reflecting the larger context of middle-class society" (1987, p. 127). Non-synergistic efforts are characteristic of individualistic societies such as the United States. In other words, our traditional health care systems are not constructed either as prosocial or as community approaches.

Native American groups, in contrast, have been characterized by their prosocial community orientations in healing. They include a conviction that illnesses such as those thought to be psychological are, in part, a product of a dysfunctional society. Native American individuals and their healers characteristically appeal to the community members' shared sense that they are all participants in the healing of each other and the community. That is, they define themselves as participants in prosocially oriented communities in which healing is a shared, empowering activity.

McCormick (1997), a Canadian First Nations member and counseling psychologist, studied whether this discrepancy between the Western, individualistic mental health orientation and the prosocial community orientation of their people might be related to their under utilization of Western mental health agencies. He interviewed fifty participants from approximately 40 different First Nations communities, including students and a variety of community members across a range of occupations. He asked them to describe how they had approached their own healing experiences. His subsequent analysis of these "Critical Incidents" focused exclusively on the actions they had taken because they embodied the core essence of the healing experience – their empowering actions to heal themselves. Three hundred ninety two (90%) of the 437 incidents reported were centered on reaching out to connect with others socially, spiritually, through traditional activities and ceremonies or participation in nature as part of all creation. While these people had also incorporated autonomous activities including self-exploration, seeking understanding of their problems, self-care and exercise, and setting goals or undertaking challenging activities, they had done so less than one-fourth of the time. Their connected rather than an autonomous sense of empowerment may have contributed to their low use of and possibly low level of interest in Western mainstream mental health services.

4.2. Organized Assaults on System Injustices and Inequities

This section shifts to an examination of single efforts to change the life contexts of entire collections of individuals such as ethnic or other non culture-defining groups (CDGs). These people are thought to be in need of assistance because of their disadvantaged situations as members of identified non culture-defining groups (NCDGs). The commonality of these efforts is that changes within existing societal arrangements are tried rather than creating new, non-hierarchical societal or community contexts. The primary concerns here are to determine what these change efforts have contributed to people's wellness and whether they have contributed to creating prosocial communities.

4.2.1. Racial and Ethnic Minorities

In the United States during the 1960s, there was a national surge of support for ensuring civil rights to African-American citizens. The situation of African-Americans as an oppressed NCDG became an important priority issue in community psychology. Some of the efforts at redressing the imbalances they faced were advanced under the headings of affirmative action, community psychology, and combinations of these perspectives.

There are many other NCDGs in the U. S. besides African Americans. They include other racial groups, e.g., Native Americans and Latinos; ethnic and religious groups, e.g., Muslims; gender preference or identity groups, e.g., gays and lesbians; and demographic groups, e.g., the homeless. We assume that the same principles apply to all NCDG efforts. However, the ones discussed below were formulated primarily on African Americans and Latinos living in the United States because there are substantial data about only these groups.

Snowden, Martinez, and Morris (1999) chose the delivery of mental health services as a focus for evaluating the contributions of community psychologists and others to the well-being of ethnic minority populations in the United States. They examined general policy level patterns, distinguishing between two broad orientations. One they called a *political perspective*. It is characterized by a belief that individual and collective forces outside of the ethnic minorities lead to their being slighted and feeling distressed. Poverty, prejudice, and being forced to live in under-served communities are considered the causal factors for the people's distress, and political changes are required to alleviate them. In contrast, advocates of a *service delivery orientation* believe that past policies toward immigrants and differences in cultural traditions lead to traditional service approaches being inappropriate and unattractive to ethnic minorities. From this perspective, solutions lie in developing culturally sensitive service systems and interventions.

Snowden et al., (1999) analyzed the current situation in which existing policies and practices lead to formulating a general diagnostic picture and then offering broad recommendations for future approaches. From their analysis, they concluded that this broad, largely context and culture-free conceptualization is counterproductive; rather, a variety of approaches are needed to address contextual and other considerations. They focused primarily on issues that had been well-researched, including the nature and extent of people's *psychological well-being and mental health*, their *social stressors* which have emphasized deficits rather than strengths, their *resources*, and *service delivery*. As they analyzed each set of issues, they made recommendations as to how ways of addressing it could be made more culturally appropriate. Their recommendations were constructive and worth implementing. However, they treated each issue as independent of the others rather than as components of a comprehensive, integrated, whole system approach. Instead, what is needed is the creation of nourishing environments and person-focused supports for the non culture-defining individuals with whom community psychologists are concerned.

Mental health well-being. The major approach for identifying mental health well-being among ethnic minorities has been the use of epidemiological studies of numbers of cases, diagnosed disorders, and treatments sought and/or utilized. These studies have established that, relative to Anglo Americans, African Americans are over represented in mental health hospitalizations, have characteristically different symptom patterns with emphases on phobic and panic disorders as well as somatization syndromes, and are disproportionately diagnosed as schizophrenic and less so as having affective disorders. Their characteristic responses to problems include denial, self-reliance, and determination. They also exhibit symptoms related to African folk beliefs and show a higher correlation between distress and use of services. In contrast, Latinos who are also vulnerable to the effects of discrimination under-utilize mental health services, particularly in the absence of bicultural and bilingual service providers.

Stress. Not surprisingly, stress is a topic of particular relevance for community psychologists who are concerned with the well-being of NCDG groups. Hostile and impoverished social conditions are prevalent in the lives of many ethnic minorities and contribute social stressors that adversely impact the people's mental health. A disproportionate number of African Americans and Native Americans experience high levels of poverty, especially those living in inner cities. In contrast, Latino populations vary more widely across socioeconomic levels, and Japanese Americans have low levels of poverty. Different immigrant groups have faced quite disparate stressful experiences, including acculturation patterns. Stressful issues include dislocation, separation from the extended family, and family disintegration arising from differential opportunities and roles in their new cultural settings. For example, those who speak English and/or have marketable skills have advantages. However, if the wives find jobs and become the primary wage earners, their increased status may become a threat to their husbands and to traditional family structures. Another particularly grave source of stress for many ethnic minorities is threats to their health and person. For example, young African American men are at particular risk for death by homicide, substance abuse, and AIDS.

Snowden et al., (1999) recommended that community psychologists' interventions be focused on stimulating constructive change through strategic social action. For example, they recommended working with specialists in public policy to develop and evaluate policy changes. Most of those recommendations include the involvement of ethnic minority individuals in productive roles in society and providing them with access to services. While these are important and worthy objectives, they provide help to a limited number of those in need.

Resources. Snowden et al., (1999) noted a recent move to explore the relationship between the quality of life of ethnic minorities and the adequacy of resources available to them. Family, religion, and indigenous healers appear to be significant resources in the lives of minorities (NCDGs). African Americans and Latinos have more contact with their families and turn to them more often for help than is characteristic of main stream United States populations. African Americans in particular often bring outsiders into their functional family and incorporate them as part of their support system.

While family dependency is at times considered unhealthy in our individualistic society, it serves as an important resource for many ethnic minorities. In fact, community psychologists could pay attention to the development of these types of constructive patterns by promoting arrangements such as small, extended family or neighborhood prosocial communities. That possibility was not noted by these authors.

Ethnic minority communities also tend to rely more on folk healers than do their CDG counterparts. Here too, Snowden and colleagues (1999) suggested that those healers offer the comfort of an intimate knowledge of the culture as well as a combined personal and professional relationship (instead of an impersonal formal one) for healing purposes. While alternative health treatments may, at times, have a negative effect on healing, the opposite may also be true. That is, the personal and ritualistic elements may promote community belongingness and group support – both important therapeutic factors in addressing psychological disturbances. These authors suggested further exploration of what these possibilities might offer.

Religion, prayer, and spiritualism were identified as key coping activities among ethnic minorities and their communities. However, those resources seem to be relatively underutilized by African Americans when they are faced with mental health problems. Snowden et al., (1999) indicated that at such times African Americans turn to family, friends, and clergy as complements, not substitutes for professional help. He and his colleagues also noted that trust and willingness to cooperate can grow from an enhanced sense of community.

Native Americans often meet as a group to heal the community and pray for the health of others, secure in the knowledge that they will, in turn, be provided the same benefits. Snowden and colleagues (1999) noted that the help-seeking behavior of connecting to others and exploring options with them may provide a powerful therapeutic effect. They suggested that community psychologists sensitize themselves to the variations of beliefs about healing and coping resources before they attempt to intervene in these or any communities.

Professionally, a problem solving approach is currently viewed as a factor necessary for successful interaction with ethnic minority communities and their residents. That is, as we primarily foster and incorporate the usual self-help approaches into the mental health approaches of NCD groups, particularly those with existing community oriented healing practices, we minimize and discourage those existing prosocial approaches which may contribute to the vitality and prosocial nature of those communities. In contrast, our entire society and mainstream community psychology could potentially advance individual and community well-being by incorporating group oriented approaches to healing as part of a prosocial community-oriented effort.

Delivery of mental health services. Snowden and his colleagues (1999) found negative ethnic biases directed toward African Americans relative to Anglos in psychiatric diagnoses, higher rates of involuntary hospital commitment, more prescriptions for medication, and less provision for individual therapy. During hospitalization for mental health problems, African American patients also receive fewer privileges and face more restrictions and seclusion. Further, they are more likely to leave treatment early. These authors emphasized the desperate need for broad and flexible evaluation of mental health service delivery in ethnic communities. (The same recommendations could be made for CDG communities). They also stressed that while ethnic minority communities, such as those in which African Americans live, tend to have members who are poorer, less educated, and less physically healthy, these communities are not all alike and delivery of mental health services to them needs to be responsive to their differences.

4.2.2. A Special Case: The Clarks' Vision and Psychology's Response

I am returning to the work of Kenneth and Mamie Clark (referred to in Chapter One) to illustrate the nature and complexity of the challenges to resolving the inequities facing all NCD and CD groups in our existing individualistically oriented system. The Clarks did not consider themselves to be community psychologists, yet they fought to create a society that would better serve all of its residents by bringing racial equity to all schools in the United States. Their goal was only indirectly related to mental health issues, and it was also only indirectly prosocial community oriented. Rather, they assumed that to create the conditions necessary for establishing prosocial communities they only needed to stimulate action at one level of society. They believed that educating people about themselves, their contribution to the injustices of their society, and how those injustices harmed them as well would lead people to change.

In *Prejudice and Your Child* Kenneth Clark (1955) emphasized that the United States is a child-centered society. Further, both Clarks, who were educational psychologists, believed that if social scientists provided people with information that demonstrated how much racial prejudice and discrimination were damaging their own children, it would lead to significant individual and social change. At least initially, they assumed that the solution to issues of prejudice was to provide all children with love, support, and accurate information during their developmental years. They felt that this type of socialization would result in the children becoming empathetic, compassionate, and humble adults who would not be filled with the anger and frustration that leads to denigrating themselves and others.

Unfortunately, the Clarks' efforts to create the awareness that prejudice and discrimination will damage the oppressors as well as the oppressed were largely unsuccessful, and their related efforts to accomplish social changes were increasingly thwarted. Kenneth Clark became more pessimistic and turned to the fields of social psychology and psychopathology to understand prejudice and discrimination (1965). He began to emphasize the need to change our social institutions to make them more supportive of social justice. Thus, the concept of organized, socially sanctioned policy and practices and the language of pathology, clinical and social, became part of the dialogue. However, even though he changed his focus, it was only to argue that change was needed at the societal level rather than the individual level.

Keppel (2002) documented that by the mid-nineteen sixties, Clark was arguing that United States society contained deep, systemic faults as reflected in the presence of ghettoes. In his view, ghettoes require and are the consequence of the CDG in a society using its power to institutionalize the powerlessness of denigrated groups. This shift in Clark's understanding of segregation as a societal problem rather than just a consequence of individuals being uninformed led to a subsequent shift on his part to address those societal problems. It also led to his later conviction that the social sciences were serving as agents of the dominant society by assisting in the retention of these strictures rather than using their work as a force for social change to eliminate them.

The year 2004 was the fiftieth anniversary of the United States Supreme Court decision to overturn their previous ruling that racially segregated schools were not discriminatory if they were otherwise equal. The ruling against that decision was based in part on social science research evidence, including the Clarks' studies with children. Their findings supported the hypothesis that segregation itself leads to feelings of inferiority among those discriminated against. That evidence was included in an appellate brief in the case of Brown v. Board of Education of Topeka. An appendix to that brief was reprinted as part of a special *American Psychologist* fiftieth anniversary issue reviewing the case and its complex consequences, (Clark, Chein, & Cook, 2004). It stressed the broader issue that "segregation, prejudices and discriminations, and their social concomitants potentially damage the personality of all children–the children of the majority group in a somewhat different way than the more obviously damaged children of the minority group" (p. 495). This latter point that beliefs and practices supporting racism also harm those in the majority was a crucial aspect of this argument. However, since that time it has been submerged and lost from social practice and in subsequent debates over the merits of the ruling.

Unfortunately, the nature of the response of the American Psychological Association (APA) and some of its prominent leaders to the historic Brown vs. Board of Education decision added substantial support for Clark's judgment. Benjamin and Crouse (2002) and Pickren and Tomes (2002) recently reviewed that APA response. Both reviews noted that this was a seminal moment in the history of psychology. It was the first time social science evidence, including some from psychology, had been used as the basis for a major decision in a court of law. He was congratulated by others who had worked to bring this issue to the Court and by African American psychologists, but he received no congratulations from his professional society. Even worse, this event was not reported on or discussed in professional meetings or in APA policy discussions between 1954 and 1956. Instead, it was largely ignored then and continues to be. Clark was still not included in a recent listing of 100 of the twentieth century's most eminent psychologists (Haggbloom, Warnick, Warnick, et al., 2002) nor is the 1954 Court decision represented as an important date in the history of psychology.

Ignoring Clark and his contribution brought an issue to psychology's attention that focused on one of its ongoing, major internal divides. Specifically, it highlighted that many psychologists believed psychology should not be socially involved; still others shared the dominant cultural view that supported segregation. The conclusion that this divisive issue contributed to APA's silence is at least indirectly indicated by APA's willingness to advocate for other public policy positions. For example, the Association has been quite outspoken about such issues as "academic freedom, freedom of scientific interchange, and the rights of psychologists in professional practice" (Benjamin & Crouse, 2002, p. 46f). In other words, it has chosen to defend the rights of individual psychologists when faced with restrictions on their societal rights. As Pickren and Tomes (2002) wrote, this same reluctance was evident in APA's refusal to place more emphasis on social problems. It was reflected in its resistance to provide more opportunities for minority students to enter psychology and for minority professionals to be more included in the organization's operation and direction. For example, an ad hoc APA Committee on Public Affairs appointed in 1966 issued its report three years later stating that the Association's highest priority should be issues of science policy and its lowest priority that of social problems (Tyler, L., 1969). Thus, the Association assigned its highest priority to protecting its rights, and its lowest to its societal obligations to advancing human welfare.

Other changes were emerging as part of the civil rights movement and were forcing consideration of related social issues. They included the broad Black Power movement across U.S. society. African American leaders within psychology also turned to other avenues to highlight social issues; one outcome was their founding of the Association of Black Psychologists. Clark (1965) thought these developments were counterproductive. He reasoned that integration was the only viable solution for resolving racial issues in this multiethnic society if there was to be equal access and social justice for all.

Pickren and Tomes (2002) detailed the subsequent important developments in opportunities for minorities (NCDGs) in the United States and in psychology. APA did respond to those pressures by establishing mechanisms to address issues of discrimination and social policy. One such mechanism was its Board of Social and Ethical Responsibility (BSERP) established in 1973 with the charge of "general concern for those aspects of psychology that involve solutions to the fundamental problems of social justice" (APA, 1973, p. xvi). However, the BSERP was, in part, also established to protect APA governance from demands of under-represented groups and other groups seeking to promote their own and other societal interests, no matter how legitimate. For example, women and Native Americans were asking for action on their grievances. African Americans had gone even further and were asking for more participation, including positions in APA's Central Office and thus in the policy and administrative direction of the Association. Pressures were mounting for APA to change not only its own, internal practices to make them more socially responsible, but also its dealings with external vendors and suppliers, including companies that provided publishing services to the Association. Again, the response focused on addressing this major social problem only at one level.

One eventual organizational response to these kinds of pressures was the establishment in the 1980s of a Board for the Advancement of Psychology in the Public Interest (APA, 1973, p. xvi). It continues to serve as an umbrella organization for addressing the concerns of disadvantaged groups; a solution that continues to produce mixed results. While it has provided institutional arrangements and resources for responding to social justice concerns, it has also maintained the ghettoization of these groups. Consequently, the APA continues to view disadvantaged groups as responsible for, if not the cause of, their inequities and their own under representation. The Board has not worked toward including these issues in the Association's and public's dialogue as matters of concern for all. Further, this Board has not linked together social and scientific concerns as inseparable facets of psychology-based undertakings. At best, the Board endorses support for diversity and an opportunity to compete for the benefits that society offers.

Fine (2004) identified three major threats to attainment of desegregation. These threats have narrowed and limited progress toward the achievement of that goal as part of the establishment of overall social equity and justice. She interviewed twelve elders, some White and some Black, who had lived through the Brown vs. Board of Education era. Based on her interviews, she identified those threats as: (a) refusing to acknowledge the enormous sacrifices the African American community made to achieve desegregation, (b) mounting overwhelming and violent resistance to desegregation by sources ranging from government officials and educators to communities and individual citizens, and (c) ignoring consideration of the damage of segregation to the White CDG. That is, instead of focusing on what the White community would gain from desegregation, its members have come more often to interpret the African American assertiveness as lack of gratitude for the White people's sacrifices made to allow these NCDGs to enter "their" CDG institutions.

Legally we have desegregation, but its goal has been defeated. Formal and informal actions to ignore or discount the responsibility of the society's culture-defining segments to participate in overcoming the harm of segregation to the entire society have triumphed. Rather than seeing desegregation as a way to transform society by creating social justice, it is considered by the white CDG as a remedial strategy for only those presumably affected, i.e., the African American children. The great African American sacrifices made in the interests of desegregation and even some of their resentment at having to educate the majority about the nature and consequences of segregation have been forgotten. The new interpretation, that African Americans are asking for special accommodations for themselves with their presumed inferior abilities and other deficits, allows for a return to the old status quo of U. S. society and rejects the necessity for prosocial changes.

This critique is not intended to say that working for individual and other social changes at only level of society is not important. That work is productive. Further, Clark's work created social changes. Nevertheless, much of Clark's broad argument that the prosocial change of integrating diverse racially defined segments of society with the rest would benefit the oppressors as well as the oppressed has been lost.

4.2.3. Addressing Inequities in the Status and Lives of Women

There has been particular attention in APA to including women as another NCD group whose members have not been accorded full participation in defining their society and the terms of their participation in it. As with racially related issues, current efforts are underway to create gender equity. They are primarily directed at helping women achieve equal status and opportunities without changing society as it exists. This orientation also ignores the possibility that women's life experiences and perceptions may be different from men's and that women might provide unique psychological insights.

Swift, Bond, and Serrano-Garcia (1999) analyzed studies about women's lives during the first quarter century (1965–1990) of the emerging field of community psychology. Their review highlighted a major problem. Many professionals had defined what are, in fact, social and certainly interpersonal attitudes and behaviors that victimize women as being "women's issues" rather than "everybody's issues". Examples of women's issues ranged from general male-female interactions to specific behaviors such as physical, emotional, and sexual abuse of women. They also included reproductive rights and care of children. Efforts to change such inequities were, consequently, often focused on the need for individual rather than system changes. Further, the professionals relied on educational approaches to change the women rather than attempting to redress existing power imbalances, remove barriers, and create resources. Consistent with that approach, these educational approaches were mainly directed at teaching the women what was wrong with them and how they could fix it.

Swift and her colleagues (1999) used Swift and Levin's (1987) four-stage formulation to identify the level of empowerment of the participants in each of the studies they addressed. Not surprisingly, the reviews found a preponderance of relatively unempowered women across a range of contexts and life conditions. Some of the research was directed at the second stage which involved examination of the institutional and structural factors that mandated women's possibilities. For example, D'Ercole and Streuning (1990) analyzed at multiple-levels the vulnerability of women to victimization through their adherence to traditional sex-role stereotypes. They then used their findings as a basis for recommending actions at the third stage of empowerment, that is, making social changes. For example, they identified ways that shelter programs could establish functional networks and build on women's strengths to mobilize their resources and protect against their victimization. Finally, Swift and her colleagues' (1999) shifted to asking whether any of the studies they reviewed reached the fourth stage of empowerment. That stage involves system openness to social change, a step only one of the reviewed studies reached.

Swift, et al's (1999) survey indicated that the number of studies which had specifically incorporated prosocial community considerations was limited. The earliest of these was reported by Gatz et al., (1982), a project in which I was a participant. We used a collaborative primary prevention approach designed to increase both community and individual competence in elderly adult community workers and the elderly adults with whom we worked. The study became one of Anglo and African American women (because of the dearth of elderly men) in 20 suburban middle class towns. Competent individuals were defined as being more internal, trusting, and actively involved in their approach to their own lives. Competent communities were defined as those characterized by higher levels of resource utilization, problem solving, communication, and influence or power channels. Such communities also offered their residents alternatives and knowledge about how to obtain and use resources.

We identified natural community leaders, then trained and employed them to promote competence in older residents identified as needing assistance. We used an initial intensive training workshop with follow-up via ongoing weekly meetings to exchange support, review activities, share information and experience, and improve worker's skills. Information was obtained from the workers, their clients, and a control group of residents. All participants showed increases in life satisfaction; African American workers and residents increased significantly in their sense of control of the events in their lives. Further, gains in a sense of personal control related positively to increased knowledge about and use of community resources (Gatz, et al., 1982).

We found that the workers acted on their own to seek increased resources for the aged in the community (Gatz, et al., 1982). That is, they empowered themselves to change the system and make it more responsive. Their actions were representative of the fourth level of empowerment. We also learned that

African American residents used informal community resources more than formal ones and did so significantly more than Anglo residents. Their participation in this project thus served them particularly well not only by broadening their community competence to make more use of their community's formal as well as informal resources, but also by using informal networks to help each other access those resources. All of these steps moved their communities in the direction of functioning together in a prosocial community fashion. It also demonstrated that these elderly women, Anglo and African American, were quite capable of contributing to the creation of more competent prosocial communities in their poorly served ones.

Rowe and Irvine's earlier review reported in Swift and her colleagues comprehensive review (Swift, Bond, & Serrano-Garcia, 1999) described a women's health center that confronted domination by its white male professionals who had maintained a traditional paternalistic, dehumanizing health care approach. The women created a team approach where professional and non-professional roles were shared. They also changed provider/client working relationships by developing new approaches that involved explaining procedures to clients, seeking the client's confirmation of diagnoses on the basis of their experiences, encouraging their questioning, their skill development, and their taking an affirmative stance. Rowe and Irwin's overall assessment was that both staff and clients were empowered by this approach.

Clinton and Larner (1988) focused on a grass-roots movement that trained local rural women to provide support services for other poor, rural families. The program's health outreach workers were mothers in similar families. They provided prenatal care for expectant mothers and follow-up services after the children were born. The outreach mothers were also engaged in becoming leaders in networks of Natural Helpers and in other capacities in their communities. Thus, in a vital way, this movement not only informed, but also helped these women empower themselves and participate in creating a more prosocially oriented community.

D'Augelli (1990) provided a relevant conceptual framework for an AIDS prevention strategy based on coordinated community planning. Although he did not focus specifically on women, his approach included them as an integral part of the community. D'Augelli described the successful development of coordinated programs to create lasting behavior change in local gay communities. They provided accurate information about adoption of behavior patterns to prevent HIV infection, skill development for such behaviors, and social support. In that sense this project acted to develop a prosocial community orientation for addressing a health crisis to which lesbians are equally vulnerable and to which they can respond in the same ways.

There have been and continue to be a substantial number of community based studies and projects which provide women a more nearly equal status and more opportunities in society. Many of them have addressed how women can change their conduct to gain more control of their lives. The changes initiated by such work have enriched the quality of those women's lives. However, to the extent that those efforts have advocated social changes, their primary emphasis has been on creating equal access, recognition, and even power for women relative to men.

4.3. The Creation of Alternative Settings

One approach tried by community psychologists and others concerned with the psychological effect of a community on its citizens is the radical solution of simply creating new settings. That is, rather than reform existing social structures, they abandoned or ignored them and tried to construct new societal arrangements and contexts. The new configurations were designed to promote the achievement of prosocial values and be task effective. Among the many alternative communities that were popularized during the past half century are the counter culture communes that sprang up and subsequently dissolved, though some have persisted. Clearly, new societal arrangements do not necessarily guarantee that such alternatives will succeed, at least not in an individualistic society. Cherniss and Deegan (1999) wrote that more attention has been paid to whether these endeavors were successful than to what kind of community innovation was established.

Comparing Cherniss and Deegan's comments and Sarason's (1972) seminal book on the creation of settings leads to a somewhat disheartening conclusion. That is, in spite of numerous efforts over the intervening 27 years to create alternative settings, we have gained little understanding of how to do so successfully. In fairness, the great post-World War II surge to be innovative, even revolutionary, was almost in its final stages at the time Sarason's book was written. Yet even today, the problems Sarason cited are still unaddressed. People who lead efforts to create alternative settings seem not to know how to create them or even what they are trying to accomplish.

Sarason (1972) suggested that those who are best positioned to create a new arrangement for a setting are those who have been involved in the old one and want changes. He suggested that successfully creating a new setting is like creating a work of art in that it involves a number of people performing together. The participants have to submerge their individuality to the creation of the desired whole. If they do so, the setting they create offers far more than the sum of its parts although the participants, including the change agents, become largely unnoticed as individuals. This kind of ongoing individual-group tension constantly changes in new settings and will never be fully resolved. Further, the changing nature of managing the process productively while continuing to build and enrich the quality of the whole production is difficult and demanding. Sarason's final assertion was that the controls of reflection and calculation should be a continual part of the process. That is, it is self-defeating to assume at any time that the problems are accurately diagnosed and adequate solutions have been found so that no further reflection is required.

Cherniss and Deegan (1999) summarized their report on alternative communities in an organized, analytic way that provides for a more nuanced analysis of the characteristics of these settings. They focused on the following general guidelines for intervention: External Relations, Leadership, The Planning Process, and Group Dynamics: Conflict vs. Commitment. Below is a discussion of each of these guidelines and a summary of the insights that we can gain from them.

4.3.1. External Relations

Alternative settings are inherently a threat to and in competition with the existing settings in their shared environment. Consequently, the survival of an alternative setting rests on its relationships with the established settings. The most effective approach for building sustaining relationships between settings is to anticipate the issues. Sarason (1972) argued that doing so requires an examination of the setting's "prehistory", including the identification of potential problems and taking steps to prevent them from arising. Goldenberg (1971) stressed that it is important for people who want to create a new setting to become reciprocally involved with people who are outside of the context and develop exchange relations. If they become involved, they create the possibility that both the old and new settings and those in them can gain without doing so at each other's expense. He also stressed the need for people in new settings to develop positive rather than negative or superior attitudes towards outsiders, both at an individual and an institutional level. Reinharz (1984) emphasized that alternative settings can have a radiating effect because they demonstrate new forms that others can consider. Cherniss and Deegan (1999) pointed out that addressing relationships with those in existing settings is "political" and often of little interest to innovators. Nevertheless, it is essential The most effective way to establish such prosocial, external relationships is for innovators to be proactive and even make accommodations to protect the integrity of existing settings. In short, employing a measure of political astuteness and involvement with those outside of the setting is an essential part of the successful development of an alternative setting.

4.3.2. Leadership

Although alternative settings may be intended to be democratic and non-authoritarian, their creation is usually led by a small group or even a single person. The characteristics that they or s/he bring(s) to that task and the nature of relationships that each leader establishes with the others are crucial factors in the success of the setting. According to Cherniss and Deegan (1999), leadership issues include the leader's self-confidence, sense of superiority or parent-like attitude, possessiveness and ownership, and "lack of sustained commitment beyond the initial stage" (p. 368). Attributes of the leader(s) that contribute to a favorable resolution of these setting's concerns include openness, candor, and support for criticism and dissent. It is also valuable to establish internal and/or external mechanisms for addressing any leadership problems, and even to specify a time-limited tenure for leaders.

4.3.3. The Planning Process

A common problem in the creation of alternative settings is the misconception that the combination of good intentions and high ideals is all that is needed. Sarason (1972) emphasized the importance of exploring all of the possible alternatives before choosing the most appropriate strategies for addressing problems that will potentially arise. Second, sufficient time must be provided for both the planning and implementing phases of the new undertaking. Third, it is essential to assess and optimize as much as possible the fit among three considerations: the setting's goals, organizational structure, and available technology. Also crucial to the establishment of an alternative setting are the selection and training processes. It is essential to select people who are comfortable with new approaches and train them to function by using the new ones being implemented. A further practical task is that of planning for adequate resources to sustain the setting and/or for incorporating resource-generating approaches such as finding volunteer talent or bartering to exchange resources with existing settings.

4.3.4. Group Dynamics: Conflict vs. Commitment

Cherniss and Deegan (1999) stressed that alternative settings tend to place high value on close, intense personal relationships if only to provide a strong sense of community. While these relationships can be highly gratifying, they also can lead to dissension that threatens the setting. Again, the best approach is to anticipate and try to prevent conflicts from arising. One mechanism is to select compatible participants. Even then, status and substantive differences can arise and lead to internal strife, the development of factions, and other counterproductive actions. Sarason (1972) focused on the importance of developing an explicit constitution of rules for governing as a crucial step in resolving, if not preventing, disruptions from weakening or destroying the setting. Cherniss and Deegan (1999) also stressed that good intentions are not enough; formal rules and procedures are needed to guide the evolution and functioning of a setting. However, "unless the setting's members are willing to confront one another openly about interpersonal problems, no formal mechanism can be very effective" (p. 374). Even in societies in which direct confrontation is taboo, people have to openly address personal as well as task issues for any setting to function constructively.

4.4. Comments

Important insights have emerged over the past thirty years from attempts to create alternative settings. They seem to indicate that doing so effectively requires a holistic approach such as that of building a prosocial community.

Trying to change one level of community functioning and expecting that its impact will spread to result in overall community change seems to be ineffective. In particular, it is crucial to organize the internal and external relationships of the setting in a prosocially oriented way. That is, all aspects of the setting must be beneficial to all concerned and, in particular, must not exploit any one segment or any individuals at the expense of others. The goals of the setting must balance task and personal psychosocial values. It is essential that the organization of the setting incorporates and involves everyone and ensures that no one is above the rules, including the leaders. Special commitment to any role in the setting does not provide a special status or separate that person from the others.

This final point seems particularly pertinent to community psychologists and other professionals. Perhaps all too often, we have stressed that our work, including our research and intervention projects, is about communities, but that we are separate from the community. We establish alternative settings, evaluate them, even write about them, but have no personal commitment beyond that. If we can opt out of any responsibility for our own role and any humanitarian concern for the well-being of the community or the continuance of the setting, so can others. A crucial core question that this approach confronts us with and demands that we answer, then, is what kind of communities do we want? We cannot create prosocial communities by focusing on specific issues. We have to take a holistic approach and acknowledge that our own involvement is required. Whether we wish to think so or not, we answer that question by how we act, not by what we say.

From reviewing the approaches that are focused on changing only one of the levels of a community's functioning, it seems that community psychologists generally believe that such a strategy will be adequate to solve or reduce the problems with which they are concerned. For example, it is now evident that external efforts to empower others can not succeed without the participation of those being empowered. While such approaches may be focused on people in need of assistance, they can only be successfully accomplished if recipients assume the responsibility to act. That is more likely to happen if individuals are approached in a collaborative way, not if, for instance, empowerment is introduced as an externally directed, one-way effort. Further, as was the case with First Nations people and other relationally oriented communities, their self empowerment approach to healing is largely prosocial community oriented.

In the review of efforts to reduce injustices toward NCD groups, Snowden and colleagues (1999) recommended that community psychologists could use epidemiological approaches to develop culturally appropriate ways to provide services. However, epidemiological approaches are not characteristically prosocially oriented; they are directed at only one level of intervention. They have been used to identify and deliver ethnically appropriate services to an ethnic group's members. However, they do not change the societal conditions that contribute to people's dysfunction or to that of the system creating their problems. Programs to reduce stress among NCD groups were similarly focused only at that level. In the same vein, practices to generate resources were considered in isolation, not as part of the fabric of the communities and related to the successful formation of prosocial communities. In the discussion about delivering mental health services, it was noted that community psychologists can potentially work with communities to identify their particular natures and possibilities, their lifestyles, and their resources. However, those service delivery approaches did not link their work to other efforts, determine whether the community was supportive, or ask whether its agencies were working collaboratively with people to include everyone in improving their well-being and that of the community. Doing so would have provided us with a basis for designing integrated prosocial community-oriented intervention approaches. These CDG community psychology efforts have been focused on only one element, e.g., eliminating inequities and injustices in the current system. There is no consideration that the system itself needs to be changed to adequately address these issues. Without adapting a holistic community approach, such an intervention by itself falls far short of improving people's lives and circumstances.

Surprisingly, during the long period of social upheaval in which the Clarks were deeply involved, the idea of developing prosocial communities never surfaced as an antidote to personal and institutional racism. Tolerance of diversity was only a muted minor key. Even the American Psychological Association Board for the Advancement of Psychology in the Public Interest has not spoken to or argued for creating a community orientation as an essential underpinning to efforts to serve the public and private interests of all of the society's citizens. Also, community psychologists have not conceptualized their organization and directed their participation to creating prosocial communities. To be comprehensive, their work should at least be directed at identifying and including the nature and role of communities and using a sense of community as the basis for understanding individual and collective human behavior. Further, community psychologists have not incorporated attention to developing and implementing ways to use that understanding to advance human well-being. At present the field is only marginally focused on this central issue. Even Clark's seminal role did not move society very far toward being more prosocial.

Any society that only accepts differences and considers its tolerance to be a sign that it is a just society, and then assigns responsibility to the disadvantaged to redress the injustices they are living with, falls short of being a prosocial community. It must go beyond that position and involve all of its members and its institutions in honoring and acting to secure the well being of everyone to meet that criterion. Results of the Clarks' and organized psychology's efforts make it clear that such a task requires a reorganizing of society as a whole, including its professional organizations and practitioners, and not just particular programs focused on creating prosocial changes at one level.

Further, although organized psychology, including community psychology, has been somewhat responsive to the issues of women's presumed inequality, responses have largely focused on providing equal treatment to individuals. It has not systematically addressed the creation of prosocial communities or other social arrangements that emphasize the well-being of all. As a consequence, these actions have implicitly supported the individualistic value system and associated societal structures that divide people within a scarcity paradigm. These endeavors have focused largely on promoting women's well-being as if it was a value in a social vacuum or as pitting women and men against each other. It has attended less to bringing women and men together to create synergistic arrangements and possibilities, for example, to consider that men and women might have different perspectives on life and the world in ways that complement each other and could potentially enrich everyone's life. The goal to establish equal rights and justice for each segment of society is a worthy goal. However, having such a goal does not guarantee that those involved will individually or in concert act to establish or maintain a prosocial community framework that not only supports their own well-being but includes that of others. It does not guarantee that individuals will move beyond these issues to establish a shared sense of concern for everyone.

As is evident in the studies presented here, innovators have not taken into consideration the nature of the human values that they and others bring with them or the nature of the contexts into which they are introducing changes. Further, change agents have not usually involved themselves in the communities or with the issues they are trying to resolve; they approach the community as outsiders without insight or commitment. That is, many of our community change approaches remain focused on trying to change one element of a community to create broader change. Unfortunately, that is a very limiting and often unsuccessful strategy.

5
The Prosocial Effect of Coordinating Change in Two Aspects of a Community

We community oriented psychologists and other change agents influence the communities where we live and work. It seems reasonable that we can do so more effectively if we first decide what kind of communities we want and then accordingly. There is a history in the professional literature that provides us some guidance about the strengths and limitations of previously completed community related projects. However, each was undertaken to create a particular kind of community, either as a desirable end in itself or as a path to accomplish other sought-after goals, but none were based on prior analyses of how communities function. To date there have been only a few attempts to analyze and restructure the nature of communities and the role of their members in maintaining or changing them. They have provided us with only limited guidance about how to accomplish our community objectives or advance our understanding of communities. We need to review those few available projects and glean what understanding we can from them.

Over three decades ago Hersch (1972) tried to identify an overarching purpose of community psychology. His view was that the field's goal should be "to improve the quality of life of the people, to promote well-being and growth, to create circumstances within which human beings can thrive, and to do these things with a spirit drawn from a foundation of democratic and humane principles" (pp. 750–751). This chapter is focused on efforts that have built on Hersch's objectives and moved beyond them toward the creation of prosocially oriented communities. That is, their creators have tried to incorporate the element of mutual concerns for the well-being of everyone in the individuals, the contexts, and their interactions. The authors of these studies and projects are people who are concerned with more than creating an equitable individualistic or adversarial society. Instead, they have tried to promote changes that benefit *both* the advantaged *and* the disadvantaged. Such accomplishments require demonstrating that an emphasis on the common good need not mean de-emphasizing individual accomplishments or viewing people's interactions as equity exchanges. Rather, they highlight how interactions can enhance everyone who is involved and the community as well. In doing so, they raise the question of whether change agents must also become engaged members of the community or whether they can remain detached from the activities and interactions they create or direct.

5.1. Prosocial Community Projects Managed by External Consultants

Intervention in a community or organization by an external consultant who provides advice and direction to solve identified problems has been one traditional community psychology role. These consultants function as outsiders who remain detached; they do not in any way become part of the organizational community that they are serving. The following examples illustrate what can be accomplished in such arrangements and what their limitations are.

5.1.1. Integration in a Productivity-Oriented Work Context

Bond (1999) used her address as President of the American Psychological Association's Division of Community Research and Action to focus on examples of community development projects that were conducted by psychologists within the United States. In general, APA's psychologists live in an individualistic society and approach their work from an individualistic rather than community oriented perspective. Consequently, when community psychologists consult with work organizations, they ordinarily do so as external consultants whose services are contracted for a particular project. The projects that Bond discussed involved diverse groups, ranging from work organizations to community organizations (voluntary and otherwise) that attempted to create a prosocial approach. In each situation, the participants were brought together to address a specified, predetermined problem such as the integration of diversity in a work, team, educational, or community context. These projects were not conducted to broadly challenge society. Instead, their efforts were directed at achieving justice, defined usually as equity or equal opportunity within a specific context.

Further, as Bond (1999) illustrated in one particular situation, societal equity was at least implicitly defined according to the world-view of the members of the dominant ethos in that context (i.e., culture-defining group [CDG] of white males). All others who were involved were from non culture-defining (NCDG) backgrounds and were alike in that they were not members of that CDG, i.e., they were not familiar with its shared but unspoken values and practice norms. They had to struggle to learn and adapt to the CDG norms in order to be accepted by the dominant group. The difficulties that the NCDG members faced were further complicated because they also differed among themselves. For instance, they did not know how and were not informed about how to work with other NCDGs in the group or with the CDGs to achieve equity. In addition, the CDGs had difficulty identifying their own explicit and implicit norms and adapting them to achieve equity or equality with those they viewed as outsiders. Usually, none of the diverse groups' views envisioned the achievement of shared resources and mutual concerns for each other. All views were based on a premise that equity means equal opportunities, not equal duties or obligations to each other and their organization or community.

From her work with these kinds of organizations, Bond (1999) identified the requirements for creating heterogeneous functional groups within communities or organizations. She built on a concept of *constructive disconnection* to enable participants to incorporate multiple realities. These "both/and" perspectives (as she called them) provided a basis for participants to believe that they could simultaneously belong to their ethnic reference group, their work group, and an overarching group such as the entire organization. That approach enabled them to reach out and build connections within their work contexts. Bond cited considerable evidence that success depended on the development of a culture of communities. Such communities must value and respect diversity with its multiple realities, connectedness with its focus on needs and demands of overall unit goals, accountability for impact on others, and a willingness to deal with being both connected and autonomous. In that process, people's existing definitions of reality have to be disrupted so they can build a new, diversity-based, and multiple reality connectedness.

Bond (1999) provided an example of a problematic work setting. She described it as characterized by individual empowerment, high job prestige, and a homogeneous work group. It led to a "a strong, monolithic team culture based on independence, focus on one's own job, scanning the environment for its impact on oneself, and the maintenance of a self-protective stance by denying any more general responsibilities in this setting (e.g., 'it's not *my* job') (p. 333). Those settings allowed few opportunities for face-to-face discussions of team issues, interdependence, or accountability to one another or the group's goals. NCDG individuals felt isolated and everyone, including management, was constrained from addressing ways to hold anyone accountable for broader issues. Consequently, there was little accountability or movement toward forming a sense of community in that type of work setting.

There are severe limitations in this example and in similar contexts for developing a prosocial community approach. Bond's emphasis on the need to create a culture of communities is consistent with the PRSC concept, but as she detailed, such settings and work cultures were not designed for doing so (1999). Further, as an outsider, her role placed her in the organizational hierarchy as an advocate for accomplishing the organization's goals which were presumably primarily about work output, not quality of life. Nevertheless, the approach of creating a culture of communities that was introduced into these kinds of situations is a step toward a prosocial community orientation with its shared concern by the participants about everyone's well-being as well as their output.

5.1.2. Protecting a PRSC from External Sanctions and Neutralizing Opponents

The three programs described in this section have been conducted by professionals who remained detached from the organizational community for whom they were consulting. However, their consultations were directed at facilitating the community oriented functioning of somewhat self-contained organizations or institutions that were situated in potentially hostile, larger societal contexts. The tolerance, if not full support, of the larger setting was required for the effective functioning of the consultee's efforts. In each of these examples, an effort was made to integrate two levels of community functioning.

5.1.2.1. A Community Rally

A succession of the Australian Motorcycle Grand Prix's yearly rallies had grown progressively violent in the face of the increasingly repressive riot-control responses of the police. Veno and Veno (1992), who respectively had backgrounds in community psychology and policing, were asked to assist in the development of a violence prevention approach to that event. While a week long motorcycle roundup might seem an unlikely context in which to form a prosocial community, they largely accomplished that goal.

Veno and Veno (1992) described their approach as "reformist" on the assumption that "positive change can occur through the altering of existing institutions and practices to create a better society" (p. 74). In this case, they tried to accomplish their goal by introducing more humane and less repressive policing tactics at the event. They began with several assumptions, namely: (1) consensus is the best form of conflict resolution; (2) situational factors need to be shaped to be conducive of peace, not conflict; (3) the human resource skills of police need to be bolstered; (4) a preventive approach to spectator violence is vital; and (5) it is essential to develop and implement an appropriate public order policy.

It is noteworthy that none of these assumptions involved directly changing the views of the rally participants. Research findings from previous rallies indicated that the participants' levels of frustration and alcohol consumption had contributed to the high levels of violence. However, in the past when policing of these kinds of public events was handled by the participants, violence was reduced. The Venos (1992) built a violence prevention policy that addressed these factors and involved both the police and motorcycle groups in working together. They arranged traffic patterns to facilitate bikers' access while minimizing disruption of other traffic. Camping areas were privatized and operators were required to be licensed and take on self-policing responsibilities. Security was developed for the campsites that relied on a marshal system worked out with representatives of the motorcycle groups. The marshals reported to a police command-center daily. In addition, observers from the motorcycle riders' community were trained by a representative from the Health Department and their own community to confront and contain sensationalist media personnel seeking to promote violence. Finally, the participants were involved in designing and implementing a comprehensive plan to evaluate the effectiveness of the violence prevention program. What this program brought together was the integration of the activities of the police, health officials, and others involved at the level of social planning with the bikers and citizens at a locality development level. The civic leaders, functioning at the social action level, did not seek to include the bikers' organization in the community nor did the bikers ask them do to so. On the other hand, they did not take action to exclude the bikers. They maintained the community's status quo, simply providing permission for the rally and extending it for future rallies, presumably because it was not destructive.

Overall, the plan was effective (Veno & Veno, 1992). There was a reduction in arrests and traffic citations. Police ratings were favorably influenced. Residents and spectators evaluated the event favorably and supported its return in the following year. From a PRSC perspective, this event demonstrated that a collaborative prosocial community that was largely self-managed and monitored could be created and sufficiently accepted by the larger community that their agencies participated in protecting it from disruptive intrusions. It was a transient community and yet one that gave evidence of being a PRSC in ways that increased the probability that it and others like it can be successfully created and protected from adverse outside pressures.

5.1.2.2. Overcoming Minority Under-Representation

Maton and Hrabowski (2004) focused on overcoming the under-representation (relative to their percentage in the population) of African Americans who receive their PhDs in natural science, technology, engineering, or mathematics (STEM) fields in the United States. They emphasized that this under representation is both socially unjust and "detrimental to society's long term vitality" (p. 547). They also noted that substantially large numbers of African American students enter college intending to major in these fields and with academic records and test scores demonstrating their highly qualified capability. Yet, once admitted, some unknown factors resulted in these students changing their majors or dropping out.

Maton and Hrabowski (2004) concluded that factors other than precollegiate preparation and students' abilities accounted for this discrepancy. They implemented a strengths-based model that "builds on the existing strengths of talented Black youth and transforms their academic and social environment" (p. 548). They focused on creating high expectations and providing appropriate environmental support. From relevant research, they identified four sets of factors as crucial to meeting those two objectives, namely: academic and social integration, knowledge and skill development, support and motivation, and monitoring and advising.

The ongoing Meyerhoff Scholars Program that Maton and Hrabowski (2004) implemented includes fourteen different components with overlapping relationships to the program's broad objectives. The support that it provides ranges from personalized monitoring to comprehensive financial support contingent on maintaining a B average. Each student is paired with a faculty mentor in a science profession. Academic and social integration are facilitated by bringing students and their families to campus for recruitment weekends and continuing to keep parents involved in social events and advised of their child's progress. In addition, support for the program is provided at all levels of the university administration. Key faculty become involved in student recruitment and selection, and many faculty provide opportunities for laboratory experiences. Added to these components are a mandatory summer program before the freshman year with courses in mathematics, science, African American Studies, and subsequent summer research internships. As part of creating a family-like system of academic and social support, all of the students live in the same residence hall during their freshman year and are required to live on campus in subsequent years. Full-time advisors are available to provide regular monitoring and support for personal and academic issues. The students are also encouraged to participate in study groups and community activities.

As part of the ongoing effort to understand the factors that contribute to the success of the program, Maton and Hrabowski (2004) studied the parenting and contextual factors related to the early academic success of the program's participants. They found that factors differ somewhat between males and females and according to household conditions, personal attributes, and other circumstances. Nevertheless, they found a characteristic configuration of relevant factors, including determined and persistent parental engagement in their children's academic performance plus strict discipline and setting of limits about right and wrong. These emphases occurred in a context of "child-focused love, support, communication, and modeling" (p. 552) plus an openness to communication about all kinds of issues. To a greater extent, the successful students tended to be surrounded and supported by extended family members, teachers, and their church community as they were growing up. Active parental support for extracurricular activities and encouragement of positive peer influences were also relevant.

The Meyerhoff Scholars Program's graduates have been five times more likely than comparable students to enter STEM area PhD programs. In Maton and Hrabowski's (2004) view, the combined influence of the program's components has contributed to this positive outcome. They noted that the program's specialized focus on African American students led to resentment, so they opened the program to other students early in its development. Still, most of the program's students are African American. While the high level of academic demands may be counterproductive for some students and divert other students from important careers such as medicine or social and behavioral science, the program has made important strides in decreasing African American under representation in the STEM fields and made other contributions as well.

Both the integrated elements of the Meyerhoff Scholar's program and the comparably integrated family and community support are appropriately characterized as prosocial community characteristics. That is, the program created contexts that support and encourage the participants to be prosocially oriented. It did so by immersing the students in activities that build on their positive attributes and potentials while nesting those activities in a prosocially oriented context rather than a self-centered and individualistic or competitive one. Participation in such prosocially organized milieus also encourages and supports comparable orientations and behavior in everyone in the project. That is, the program encourages everyone from the university administration to the faculty, staff, the students, their families, and other students, to behave prosocially.

This program's stated goals are to provide an opportunity for its students in the STEM fields and to provide for a more representative set of participants in the broader STEM enterprise. Maton and Hrabowski (2004) argued that these potential scientists and leaders will add to a larger, highly educated, influential Black leadership in society. These educators (Maton & Hrabowski, 2004) pointed out that they also have an additional objective. They are disseminating their work to a wide audience including policy makers, educators, parents, and children, by "highlighting the positive academic potential of Black youth and countering the negative stereotypical images that too often dominate public attention" (p. 548). The worth of the specific goals of their program and its social change objectives seem to have been well validated.

Those are important and worthwhile goals, and adopting a collaborative prosocial structure and processes at the social planning and locality development levels to accomplish them provide substantial support for the value of this approach. However, from a prosocial community perspective the program has several limitations. Specifically, it does not (a) contribute to creating a broader, more comprehensive, prosocial community oriented society, or (b) lessen the need to protect prosocially oriented students and programs from intrusion by those who would oppose them in order to advance their own individualistic or controlling objectives. This program was designed to solve a specific problem in society and demonstrated its effectiveness at doing so, but its impact was limited in that it was not designed to change the conditions that create such problems. That is, this program engaged the students' families and others with the students in helping them to become resourceful participants in their education rather than marginalized individuals in need of assistance. However, it has been sustained at the social action level as a special program rather than as an integral part of a prosocial university community structure for all of its programs.

5.1.2.3. Addressing a Particular Problem of Concern

Extending over nearly two decades, Olweus (1991) developed and evaluated a Bullying Prevention Program. He did not set out to create prosocial communities nor to become involved in them, but his research led him to construct a program that is most commonly referred to by educators as a "whole school approach" (Rigby & Bagshaw, 2003). Olweus' program is built on the PRSC strategy of incorporating everyone in each setting by addressing the problem of bullying in a mutually supporting way rather than isolating the bullies and their targets and focusing on them as perpetrators and victims.

Olweus was concerned with understanding the roots of prosocial and antisocial behaviors, particularly antisocial aggression. In the 1970s, he began studying bullying/victim problems in Scandinavian schools, defining bullying as intentionally inflicting, or attempting to inflict, injury or discomfort on another. By the 1980s, he had found that among students from ages eight to sixteen, approximately 6% to 7% engaged in regular bullying of other students and approximately 9% of that sample were victims. His early research had indicated that two types of factors are important in the development of these problems in individuals. They are: 1) "personality characteristics or typical reaction patterns, in combination with physical strength or weakness in the case of boys", and 2) "environmental factors, such as the attitudes, behavior, and routines of relevant adults–in particular, teachers and principals" (Olweus, 1991, p. 14).

These findings led Olweus (1991) to develop bullying prevention programs that incorporated attention to both sets of considerations. The programs were built on several key principles:

> First, create a school (and home) environment "characterized by *warmth, positive interest, and involvement from adults*".
>
> Second, create a school (and home) environment characterized by "*firm limits to unacceptable behavior*".
>
> Third, "in cases of violations of limits and rules, *nonhostile, non-physical sanctions* should be consistently applied". Included also are *monitoring* and *surveillance* in and out of school.
>
> Fourth, "*adults* are supposed to *act as authorities at least in some respects*" and serve as positive role models. (p. 443)

A set of activities to create awareness and involvement and measures of both were developed to implement these principles. They were introduced at the level of the school, the class, and the individual. The program involved teachers and staff, bullies and their victims, their parents, and the other children in the school. Activities included making school playgrounds more attractive, creating teacher groups to develop better classroom climates, establishing class rules and sanctions against bullying plus praise for prosocial behavior, cooperative learning, common positive activities, serious talks with bullies and other children with and without their parents, and discussion groups with the parents. Emphasis was placed on increasing everyone's awareness of and knowledge about bullying/victim issues, actively involving parents and teachers, and providing support and protection for the victims (Olweus, 1991).

Olweus (2003) found that by 2001 the numbers involved in bullying in the society had grown by sixty five percent and the number bullied by fifty percent. In his view and that of his colleagues, the increase was because of the society's changing social conditions. By that time, research and holistic community programs in numerous other countries had addressed this serious and apparently growing problem in similar ways by adapting Olweus' program to their local conditions. Although it was implemented in a range of countries, its core elements were retained. Over time, Olweus' approach has been found to be effective in reducing bullying and related behaviors in any location where it is used, even as bullying increased in the society overall. The principles and the patterns of implementing them endorsed the creation of a prosocial collaborative link between the social planning and locality development levels in these communities and a prosocial sense of individual conduct on the part of everyone involved at those two levels.

Still, there were problems associated with Olweus' efforts. Victims were more protected, but more likely to be helped at school than on the way to and from home. In addition, the parents of bullies and their victims were more reluctant than others to participate (Olweus, 1992). Rigby and Bagshaw (2003) noted that in individualistic Australia, there was more resistance to adopting this approach than in, for example, Norway. Also, they found that among young adolescents (middle school years in the USA), a substantial percentage of students were skeptical of the teachers' interest in and skill at controlling bullying, and thus more resistant to the teachers' involvement. This approach was used in many settings and designed to be implemented by each school site rather than by an active consultant who immersed him/herself in all of the participating school systems. We are left not knowing how having an involved person to guide the implementation of this approach could have affected these efforts. Such difficulties suggest that further study is needed to identify what the minimal requirements are for guiding the installment of a prosocial community-oriented approach in community based institutions such as the schools. However, it demonstrated that including the community at a locality development level in conjunction with social planning changes in the school system and other relevant agencies did successfully reduce the incidence of antisocial aggression and facilitate the development of prosocial interactions, particularly among school children. As with the other projects, these programs did not lead to substantial prosocial social action changes in the societies in which they were implemented.

5.2. The Prosocial Effect when Consultants Become Involved

A crucial step in creating a context in which teams will work across differences within organizations or communities is shifting the focus and arrangements in projects. That is, fostering interdependence, team accountability, defined goals for the enterprise, and sensitivity to the impact of members on each other can be transformative. All CDG and NCDG members also need to be made aware of their interdependence and learn that being inclusive is to their mutual benefit. Because consultants are more likely to have the perspective and skills to foster these developments, they often assume or are assigned the role of facilitating changes, but doing so requires that they become engaged with the community. Traditional views must be disrupted to permit the creation of successive, self-renewing relationships that connect workers across newly legitimized multiple perspectives. For example, people's multiple realities and differences are embedded in circumstances that have rendered some of the people less visible than others. As mentioned earlier, that situation must be changed so that all of the participants can grasp that there is not just one way to view or do things and that having "both/and" perspectives is of superior value.

Over time, the ongoing development of mini-prosocial communities within the broader cultural context of individualism are needed to stimulate and model the nature and benefits of a prosocial orientation. However, the individualistic focus on identity and autonomy which permeates psychology, as well as almost everything else in the communities and societies of the Western world, inevitably limits and usually defeats such efforts. Individualistic sameness means keeping the status quo by treating everyone as though they are alike. In contrast, a PRSC perspective means treating each person in the particular way that leads to his/her getting a fair share of resources and a sense of interdependence and connectedness. In order to create and sustain even small PRSCs within larger, individualistic societal contexts, those involved have to continue protecting their established PRSCs until they can become largely self-contained units. The review of the projects described in the rest of this section is focused on those two concerns and a third one. That is, we will also examine how and whether small prosocial community oriented projects can eventually change the larger contexts in which they are nested.

5.2.1. Resolving a Major Community Conflict

This first example is particularly clear about the necessity for change agents to become at least limited members of a community and acknowledge their investment in it in order to create a prosocial community orientation. Although it was not their original intent, Bishop and Syme (1992) found it necessary to assume at least limited membership in a rural Australian community. They had expected to be involved only to investigate and recommend potential actions to resolve a major community conflict. They found that if they assumed a detached role, it would effectively end their efforts and prohibit accomplishment of their contractual goals. As they described the dilemma they faced, the "methodological and theoretical issues raised. . . .include the risks involved in participant conceptualizing, allowing methodology to evolve during the research process, substantive theorizing [considering context], ethics, and the importance of history in influencing realistic roles for psychologists" (p. 93). That is, Bishop and Syme could not maintain a detached outsider position and manage all of the aspects of the project process and meet their goals. They had to acknowledge that the project belonged to the community. They could jump in and help guide the process or they could stay apart and admit failure. They decided to become engaged with the community by combining the roles of collaborator, participant-conceptualizer, and citizen of the community itself in order to carry out the project.

They had been asked by the regional development authority of a small shire (county) in southwest Australia to "address what the community should aim towards by the end of the century in the face of imminent social change". Issues included "housing, tourism, the environment, land use and settlement patterns, arts and culture, social services, services for youth, and employment, industry and commerce" (Bishop & Syme, 1992, p. 94). The original plan was to gather relevant data through a series of workshops and make a set of recommendations to the community. That approach proved ineffective because of the diversity and consequent conflicts in the community. Those conflicts were primarily due to differences between the traditionally conservative primary producers and small business people and the more environmentally conscious "greenies". The former were longer term residents who had endured privation and endorsed it as legitimizing their view. The latter, who had arrived more recently, were a combination of more affluent people and some recently arrived and less affluent, counter-culture activists.

Initially, the research team planned to interview only those in each group who were directly involved to provide a data base to inform their recommendations (Bishop and Syme, 1992). However, once they started they were soon overwhelmed by requests for community input and by the heat of the conflict. They revised their approach, collected opinions from all sides on the housing issue, and then persuaded the opponents and relevant agencies to discuss the findings. They also met with and involved the leaders of the various factions in using existing formal and informal community processes to work out an acceptable solution.

They revised their research approach to allow for more flexibility and responsiveness. Archival data were collected and analyzed to enable them to better respond to these issues in light of the community's history. Community group surveys focused on the groups' and people's histories, roles, and organizational patterns, the futures people expected in and for their group and the community, and other issues that needed addressing.

The research team then focused on their broader objective of providing guidelines for community development (Bishop & Syme, 1992). Meeting this objective required that they be seen as equally open to hearing both sides. They could not sit back and reserve judgment; they had to provide feedback and recommendations to everyone as issues and ideas emerged. Recommended actions were limited to those that the community judged to be achievable. A discussion document was prepared and circulated as a basis for small group workshops designed to examine the issues, problems the community presented, resources needed, potential solutions, and who would be responsible for change.

Results of these workshops were used as a basis for findings and recommendations which were presented to the Shire (County) Council, the Director of the Regional Authority (sponsor of the project), and the local press. This meeting accomplished several goals. It enabled the Council and others to express their views openly to the research team and get their reactions. That dialogue, in turn, allowed the Council members to work through their feelings and differences, move on to a careful examination of the report, and consider how they could build on it in the interests of the community. The meeting also enabled the Council and, at least indirectly, the community to take ownership of the report and ask the research team to help with planning its implementation.

This approach presented some atypical problems for the research team. By becoming participant conceptualizers, they had become members of the community to some extent. For example, once they became engaged, they were reluctant to ask directly for feedback on the effectiveness of their work since they did not want to be seen as seeking congratulations. They turned primarily to public media such as newspaper reports to examine how effectively they had followed their own ethical guidelines (Bishop & Syme, 1992).

Further, Bishop and Syme had traded controlling power for collaboration and enabled the community and its members to empower themselves and also become collaborators. Consequently, as they expressed it, "the methodology developed as the project developed. The process of self-reflection on the part of the researchers as information was received was an integral part of our participant conceptualization. It has its costs for we were vulnerable to mistakes and criticisms by the community even when we were convinced we were right" (Bishop & Syme, 1992, p. 106). Further, "the nature of the research itself was a vehicle for community participation" (p. 107). This shift to collaborative participation with the community became an integral part of the process enabling them to achieve the project's objectives.

As reflected in these psychologists' retrospective view, they had achieved at least two major outcomes. First, their work led them to identify how they and the community needed to proceed to resolve the issues confronting them. In addition, they began to shift from being traditional, objective observers to becoming participant conceptualizers. They embedded themselves in the community and worked collaboratively with it to make it a prosocial community. The approaches that they used were highlighted in the principles they drew from the project.

From a broader perspective, this project illustrates why the community participation of change agents is needed if they are to successfully participate in formulating and influencing change. Change agents can help guide powerful and powerless segments of the community move toward constructive solutions that are responsive to everyone's issues. For example, they can use dialogue and the research processes to persuade them to accept conflict as healthy and to respect and resolve their differences. That is, change can be accomplished only by creating a 'resilient community' that can tolerate diversity of opinion. A more specific consequence is that the community's goal can shift from seeking utopian solutions to working out ways of managing conflicting and competing demands that take into account the community's history and coping strategies.

A successful community needs a code of ethics that is consistent with its overall well-being rather than one that is individualistically oriented. In particular, change agent leaders must adopt and follow that code. In this instance, Bishop and Syme (1992) followed and advocated two general rules of justice formulated originally by Rawls (1971). First, "the greatest equal liberty principle" holds that each person and group is entitled to the greatest individual liberty consistent with supplying the same freedom for others. Second, social and economic inequities are addressed in ways that are to everyone's advantage, particularly those least well off, and those imbalances are attached to positions to which everyone can aspire equally.

Bishop and Syme's approach built on Rawl's principles in ways that enabled the residents to begin investing in their community and come to see it and themselves as prosocial. It became what these psychologists called a *resilient community*. Although Bishop and Syme (1992) had not begun the project with that objective, they learned that they had to develop a framework for the community and its members continued joint prosocial functioning. Unfortunately, there were two important limitations to their ad hoc approach. They had not explicitly worked out for themselves and with the community a way to meaningfully withdraw their membership, nor had they considered how the community could continue to fill their role in ways that would help sustain its prosocial functioning. Thus, although this approach successfully combined locality development, social planning, and even some social action elements as the civic leaders assumed ownership of the project and sought to carry it out, it fell short of creating the social action changes of establishing a formal collaborative prosocial structure and self-governing processes to sustain itself as a prosocial community. A prosocial community cannot survive without sustaining its ongoing investment in the well-being of the entire community and maintaining community processes and leadership to serve that purpose.

5.2.2. Creating an Alternative Setting

Goldenberg (1971) reported on his work with the Residential Youth Center (RYC) and its program in New Haven, Connecticut. It was designed to create a setting that would provide a supporting framework for addressing individual and social limitations and inequities facing inner city youth. That is, the Center was to provide a context for the development of prosocial community-oriented endeavors, an approach very different from what was usually followed in that kind of environment. Consequently, this alternative setting project is discussed in more detail here than was the case in Chapter Four because the RYC project focused on changing more than one level of society as its goal.

The RYC was undertaken as an experimental and demonstration project supported by funds from the United States Department of Labor as part of its War on Poverty. That agency's guiding belief was that the needs of the poor could be met by creating a variety of "opportunity" programs to enable them to break out of their self-perpetuating cycle of poverty and become part of "the so-called mainstream of American life" (Goldenberg, 1971, p. 117). Locally, the RYC was administered through Community Progress, Incorporated (CPI), a community action agency formed to "fulfill the needs of New Haven's poor" (p. 20) and carried out in conjunction with Yale University's Psycho-Educational clinic.

This project was created as an alternative setting within a manpower-oriented center to evaluate the degree to which its innovative approach could facilitate the rehabilitation and development of disadvantaged youth and their families. That goal is laudable and their achievement was impressive. Most instructive here is what the project's participants, structures, and processes can tell us about the formation, nature, and role of prosocial communities. Therefore, a number of aspects of this program are described in the following paragraphs.

The Design. The local youth included in the RYC program were selected using ratings based on pooled judgments from a variety of community agencies familiar with them. The RYC opened by taking in the 20 male youths between the ages of 16 and 21 judged to have the "greatest number of problems and the longest histories of social, vocational, educational, and personal failure" (Goldenberg, 1971, p. 395). The 20 youths who ranked next worst on those criteria were chosen to serve as a control group. Both groups of youth were then tested, assessed, and interviewed on *behavioral* (work, income, and community behavior, i.e., involvement with the law) and *attitudinal* (perceptions of self and society, alienation and trust, skills at manipulating the world) measures. Follow up testing occurred after 6 and 12 months with participation in the RYC program serving as the experimental intervention.

Results were compiled for *vocational functioning*, *attitude change*, and *community behavior*. Although they were highly complex, the overall patterns can be summarized. The work opportunities available to most of the youth in both groups were with CPI's Basic Work Crews (an elementary supervised experience combining work and remedial education). Vocationally, the RYC youth improved in work attendance, attained higher work status, and increased their income levels. Attitudinally, they became less alienated and authoritarian, Machiavellian but no less trusting, and adopted a more positive world view. The Controls tended to remain unchanged or drop to lower levels vocationally. They became more alienated, unchanged in authoritarianism and Machiavellianism, less trusting, and more negative about the world. With regard to community behavior, the RYC youth showed significant decreases in number of arrests and time spent in jail during this period while the Controls changed in the other direction. Thus, the RYCs had worse records on both measures before the study began, but had improved to be significantly better than the Controls by the six month point of the study. The RYC experience seemed to have a much needed, powerful, personal and prosocial impact (Goldenberg, 1971). What underlay that experience, what was it like, how did it work, and what were its limitations?

The inspiration. The RYC program's organization grew, in part, out of its effort to create an alternative to what were seen as the self-defeating growth patterns in the CPI, the parent organization that was incorporating more and more community-oriented programs (Goldenberg, 1971). With its growth, CPI was shifting away from its innovative, experience-based way of working and becoming a more typical, hierarchical bureaucratic organization. Credentials, job titles, and formal duties began to supplant in importance people's intrinsic interest in their work and their ability to relate to and work with inner city people and their problems. It was becoming an organization in which individuals were expendable and replaceable, and the community residents were viewed as clients with problems, not people struggling with difficult circumstances.

RYC's project designers concluded that meeting its central goal would require the creation of an appropriate organization and setting. A context was developed to foster the kinds of behavior in the people conducting the program that were the same as the desired goals for the participants. Otherwise put, "if people, regardless of their background or levels of formal preparation, were involved in what for them were meaningful, intrinsically gratifying, and growth-producing human service activities, the results could not help but be beneficial to the clients with whom they were engaged" (Goldenberg, 1971, p. 124). As Goldenberg later summarized, "we were, for better or worse, engaged in the process of creating a community–not a therapeutic one in the narrow sense of the term, and certainly not one devoted solely or primarily to meeting the needs of its 'clients', but a community that would enable *all* its members to participate in a series of extended growth experiences" (p. 152). They undertook the creation of a fully collaborative, open-ended, growth oriented program which was consistent with and could accomplish their desired goals.

They set out to create a prosocial community rather than creating prosocial elements within the traditional RYC program structure. They formed a horizontal organization in which the staff could

> (1) learn from one another in a situation characterized by reciprocity and mutuality; (2) develop a clinical sensitivity and perspective that was both individually and collectively helpful; (3) pursue and retrieve the kind of training that would facilitate the assumption and utilization of personal responsibility; and (4) work and live in an atmosphere of interpersonal openness and trust. (Goldenberg, 1971, p. 127f).

RYC did have an official organizational structure and job titles, primarily to provide external legitimacy. However, the program was designed to erase the distinction between staff and clients as being two different kinds of people and to do so similarly among the staff. Everyone–staff, clients, clients' families–was to be regarded as a person with troubles and as trying to find meaning, relatedness, and a sense of competence in a sometimes incomprehensible world. Each individual came to be seen as a resource as well as a person in need of other resources. All staff shared job functions including administrative duties, clinical responsibilities, housekeeping activities, and live-in supervisory duties.

Most of the staff, the clients, and their families had previous experiences with society's formal help and control systems and had been alienated by those interactions. Thus, everyone's participation included their shared belief in the need for a different approach and their willingness to take the risks involved to create an alternative setting, a prosocial kind of community. It was to be a community where staff and clients could work together and facilitate the development of a more constructive sense of individual responsibility within their lives and relationships. Consequently, the staff members' way of viewing themselves and others and interacting with them was considered to be more important than any particular skills and credentials they might possess. It was commonly assumed that they could accomplish their goals only by instituting a community that "would enable *all* of its members to participate in a series of extended growth experiences" (Goldenberg, 1971, p. 152).

The process. The RYC adopted a variant of sensitivity group training to create the kind of community that was envisioned as essential to accomplishing their goals (Goldenberg, 1971). It enabled people to share their problems in closed, confidential group meetings among the staff, the residents, and various combinations of both. However, the participants were not strangers and they were not meeting in an isolated context. The few professionals and the more numerous non-professionals met as part of their ongoing organizational activities with the group leader who was also part of the organization and subject to the group process. The participants knew that the problems they faced could never be solved but could be worked with if they were faced openly and regularly in a self-reflective and self-correcting way. Everyone would necessarily be involved in interactions and some would have clinical problems. All would have to develop some clinical sensitivity and skills. Fortunately, doing so would enhance their ability to see themselves through the eyes of others and develop everyone's personal competence and interpersonal effectiveness along with the group's cohesiveness. Finally, this approach enabled them to acquire research data that would provide a record to prevent them from getting trapped by their own history. Overall, they judged that the most important function that these group meetings served for RYC was to enable people to talk among themselves "without fear and without regrets" (Goldenberg, p. 220).

The complexities of change. The interlocking goals of the RYC included focusing public resources on how to construct a setting and process that would result in solving major problems (Goldenberg, 1971). The RYC's concern was with the problems faced by the inner city poor within the affluent society of the United States. Their approach assumed that the goals could be accomplished only by engaging everyone in a shared effort to find common purpose in their humanity and to work together on the basis of trust and openness.

In evaluating the impact of this approach it is important to ask how the staff and RYC's ways of functioning changed and how those differences affected the staff. Some of the relevant answers are largely impressionistic (Goldenberg, 1971). The staff was initially skeptical of their ability to function clinically, but they increasingly came to value, enjoy, and feel competent in their growing abilities as they saw improvements in the youths with whom they worked and heard the supportive judgments of their colleagues. In contrast, they initially felt confident that they could undertake administrative duties, but never came to view administrative duties as intrinsically gratifying. Overall, the staff developed a strong sense of personal ownership of the setting and even invested their "free" time in it (Goldenberg, 1971). In that sense, their approach did seem to create for them a sense of belonging to a prosocial community.

Unfortunately, the staff's commitment to personal ownership of the RYC created conflicts with the surrounding community, i.e., CPI, the Psycho-Educational Clinic, and the federal administration (Goldenberg, 1971). At times those agencies either would not or legally could not respond to anyone except formally designated individuals such as the Director. This issue effectively disallowed the legitimacy of everyone else. Another difficulty rose with regard to the families of staff, particularly wives, who felt increasingly left out as their spouses became more immersed in the RYC program. Structural problems such as formal status and income differentials created friction over perceived differences in work load (versus status and income). Lower status workers sometimes had larger case loads than supervisors, so they questioned their lower pay.

Even if the participants had desired to change these external constraints and known what kind of change they wanted, the controlling agencies would not have permitted them. As Goldenberg noted, the War on Poverty was not set up to change society; the RYC program was. In that regard, the RYC was unable to solve the problem any such alternative setting faces. That is, the problem of how to relate to and protect itself from the intrusion of potentially destructive outside forces. Overall RYC's effect on its broader context was uneven at best (Goldenberg, 1971).

It is also important to know whether the staff was changed in ways that provided personal and professional growth for them. Without longitudinal data, that question could not be answered. The staff did regress to a desire for authoritative leadership in decision making when crises arose. On the other hand, pre-post questionnaire data indicated that the staff generally became less alienated over the twelve month period studied. A number of staff did move on to advanced positions in RYC and other agencies. As noted above, one of the external constraints on this type of development was the social structures designed to resist upgrading of personnel without traditional educational credentials (Goldenberg, 1971).

Summary of Residential Youth Project. The synopsis presented here is only a sketchy account of what was a most thoughtful, insightful, and self-conscious, comprehensive attempt to change a context and its people. The objective was to overcome the chronic systemic, personal, and interpersonal destruction of disadvantaged youth and RYC staff. This project began by assuming that what transpires in any situation is a product of its people, their processes of interacting, and the structure itself. Consequently, people must collaboratively change themselves, their processes, and that structure or they will work against themselves, each other, and their goals. The change process has to be a holistic one in which the change agents who lead it become an integral part of it. In fact, they can only lead by becoming as open to change and as vulnerable as the others. In that way, they model the collaborative prosocial effort.

The RYC project was of a limited scope, and the empirical findings in support of its validity were tentative. However, it confirmed that working with markedly alienated and antisocial individuals does have an individual and collective prosocial growth effect. The project provided substantial support for the belief that the interpersonal dynamics of the participants were indeed central to its success. The approach that provided a basis for trust and openness in communication among all of its members without regard to their roles or status was the creation of a context and mechanism (sensitivity groups) for addressing those dynamics.

Overall, RYC's seminal importance is far greater than its specific accomplishments and limitations. Its noteworthy achievements included pioneering an approach that stands as a unique model for the potentials and problems of such an undertaking. Although it illustrated that creating a prosocial community is theoretically possible in a difficult context, in reality only its social planning and locality development undertakings were successful. What finally led to its demise was the difficulty in this particular context of developing and implementing social action policies that could sustain it and resist the countervailing pressures of the surrounding context in which it was nested.

Even so, the RYC had a demonstrable prosocial impact on the youth who were enrolled. It also provided an experience that enabled several of its staff to advance to positions of greater responsibility and leadership in other agencies. These individuals then had an opportunity to create new settings and programs with similar prosocial approaches and objectives. That is, their RYC participation had provided them with the capacity for continued professional growth as role models and leadership for helping to create prosocial approaches in other environments. Also demonstrated was that *participants*, including the *policy makers* and *leaders*, in a prosocial community effort *have to become involved*; they cannot remain detached. Everyone must participate openly and become vulnerable as individuals as well as in their official capacities. To create a new setting, *everyone must acculturate* just as people do when they immigrate to a new culture. In this instance, outside forces more than the participants' resistance to prosocial community assimilation hampered the RYC's development as a prosocial community.

5.3. Relevant Efforts

Probably no one has invested as much thought and effort as Sarason to learning how to create new settings and enterprises and then sustain and realize the initial hopes and energies generated in them. He has consistently focused on ways to change society in order to reduce human miseries and improve the quality of people's individual and collective lives. As the Director of the Yale Psycho-Educational Clinic, he was a significant figure in the creation and operation of the Residential Youth Center project and a mentor of Goldenberg. Sarason discussed at length the creation of the RYC and Goldenberg's unique role in it as part of his 1972 book about creating alternative settings. His central thesis was that most approaches to creating alternative settings and analyses of those settings were based on a utopian perspective. Critiques of them have, in turn, focused on those settings as though they were supposed to be fully formed utopias. Little attention has been paid to examining the processes of their formation. Consequently, the critiques have ignored the actual detailed nature and history of each setting, where it was installed, the history of the people creating it and of those for whom it was purportedly intended, and the process itself. No critiques took into account that the involved people may have brought the flaws with them that doomed the setting. The creators of those settings did not view themselves as part of the setting and as needing to be as open to change as others in it. Sarason argued that for these reasons, the problems they identify and set out (largely unsuccessfully) to resolve, proliferate as do the programs and professionals.

Sarason (1972) emphasized that people who are involved in ongoing efforts to create social change need to be personally engaged in them in order to gain general knowledge and to become educated and proficient at using needed professional and research skills. He rejected the conventional wisdom that both knowledge and skill should or could be acquired from a stance of detachment and isolation from involvement in the ongoing reality. Sarason focused on creating new settings because he believed that their nature determines much of what happens and what can be accomplished in them. He also believed that people's interactions are important attributes of a setting, so he emphasized the value of creating resource networks as a vehicle for prosocial changes.

Sarason provides a useful reminder that, although projects such as those discussed here are flawed, they make important steps forward.

> Wherever new knowledge and understanding will take us is not predictable. It is hard to accept the fact that the more you know the more you need to know and that it is an endless procession that does not end in a utopia. There will always be problems. This is the consequence of all new knowledge just as it should be part of the perceived reality of all those who create settings today and dream of future societies. (Sarason, 1972, p. 284).

Sarason (1972) left us with what he sees as an insoluble problem. He argued that the core dynamics of resource networks can function only in informal networks, not formal ones. He felt that if those involved try to create formal structures, they will defeat their purpose. At the same time, he viewed formal bureaucracies as being opposed to the creation and spread of resource networks. That dilemma must be resolved if anyone is going to successfully create communities that can maintain themselves while also retaining their capacity for creativity and self-renewal.

Creating and sustaining prosocial communities and people who value them is a never ending process. Doing so requires creating interrelationships between formal and informal organizations (networks) within communities and across entire societies. It also requires involving all elements of a community in a shared commitment to nurturing the well-being of others as well as themselves and the prosocial community structure and processes.

5.4. Comments

In this chapter, we can again include Alan and Beth as active participants in their own lives and in shaping their life contexts. It may seem artificial in closing this chapter to try to imagine Alan and Beth placed arbitrarily in each of these settings, but doing so highlights how different contexts impact on new people thrust into them. What they can do and how they are changed will differ in different contexts. How the people in the situations are affected by their presence will also depend both on them and the nature of the context. Further, those interactive effects are likely to have the greatest impact on the new people entering the situation, particularly young people who are just forming their adult psychosocial competence styles.

In some of these programs, Alan and Beth would have been accorded active agent status for themselves but not as full participants. They did not seek careers in the STEM field's program of Maton and Hrabowski, but had they done so they would have been incorporated into a supportive prosocial environment. However, they would not have been included as active participants in shaping that community. In contrast, had they been assigned to teach in a school which had a bullying prevention program of the type Olweus had developed, they would have been included in creating a prosocial and supportive environment and been active participants in carrying out the program.

In their present life situations, Alan and Beth would not be participants in or influenced by the types of work situations Bond described or settings such as the motorcycle rally on which Veno and Veno focused. However, new participants in those situations would be accorded an active role in managing both their own roles and the process of solving the problems those groups faced. As new teachers, had Alan and Beth gone to the Australian community where Bishop and Syme were involved, they would immediately have been eligible to participate and contribute their unique perspectives as full participants in the community and in solving its problems. Finally, they would have been most fully engaged had they participated directly in Goldenberg's RYC program and, at least peripherally, if they had become teachers in the inner city schools that interacted with that program. However, it was the formal rules and roles of external local and federal agencies interacting with the RYC's prosocial community orientation that presented the most substantial threats to Alan and Beth's and their students' personal and professional development.

In spite of the somewhat uneven development of these programs and their limitations, it seems evident throughout these projects that their prosocial community attributes strengthens them and enriches the potential benefits that Alan and Beth can receive from participation in them. Creating a milieu in which all of its participants are respected and viewed as resourceful contributors provides more possibilities for new people like Alan and Beth to contribute to and gain from them. Further, those interactive effects are likely to have their greatest impact on the new people entering the situation, particularly young people who are just forming their adult psychosocial competence styles. Calling attention to them focuses us again on the reality that the people in and those entering any context do so as complex and diverse individuals with distinctive histories and natures.

6
A Guide for Establishing Prosocial Communities

Many communities are not organized to provide a rewarding quality of life for all of their people, nor if they do reach that goal, can they sustain or enhance that quality over time. The initial section of this chapter summarizes reasons for using the Transcultural Ethnic Validity/Prosocial Community formulation as a model when seeking to meet and sustain prosocial goals in community development. That conclusion rests on the fact that this prosocially oriented approach is responsive to factors that, when ignored, have led to failures such as those mentioned in the earlier chapters. That is, it rests on a different, overall perspective about individuals, their communities, and their interrelationships.

As we have seen in the previous chapters, past approaches to community development have characteristically been designed to change one aspect of either individual behavior or of a community or society's mode of functioning without taking the broader context into consideration. Such narrowly focused efforts to change individuals, no matter how well conceived, often led to unexpected outcomes and failures because they ignored the contextual factors. Similarly, contextually based endeavors have yielded undesirable outcomes because they did not consider the characteristics of the involved individuals. It is now time to look closely at the details of the Prosocial Community model and understand how it directs our thinking and expands our entire approach so that we consider both the context and the individual.

This Chapter describes how this action-integrated framework supports the creation of prosocial communities. To accomplish that objective requires developing and using two sets of approaches in coordination with each other. The first set is directed at (a) facilitating the perspectives and skills required to understand the nature of a prosocial community, and (b) integrating its program development activities in the three levels of development, i.e., locality development, social planning, and social action. The second set of approaches is focused on (a) conceptualizing and developing coordinated activities (psychosocial competence patterns) that respond to the perspectives, capabilities, and needs of the individuals involved (i.e., ethnically valid), while also (b) facilitating the development of the contexts in which they live in a way that is (c) encouraging of peoples' conduct and their programs to adopt and implement a resource exchange and enhancement style that will build a prosocial community.

6.1. Three Levels of Action

In Chapter Two I described three basic levels of action (social action, social planning, and locality development) that need to function in concert for us to construct and sustain prosocial communities. Although past and current community development efforts have sometimes referred to one or two of these areas of concern, it is essential that actions at all three levels be simultaneously developed or the project or program is not likely to last. Because of their frequent central importance, we need to revisit these three action levels. Briefly, *social action* refers to policy activities of civic leaders. *Social planning* is professional and management activities to implement policies on behalf of the community. *Local action* is the individual and shared activities of citizens to solve the problems they face in their lives in the community. To make it clear what each part adds, it is useful to first describe them separately in order to highlight the strengths and limitations of each level. We can also then see how to facilitate the prosocially oriented development of each part. Most of the attention in the literature has been paid to social planning activities, perhaps not surprisingly since social action and social planning are where the behavioral, social, and health sciences and professions direct their programmatic energies. For that reason, I will discuss social action and social planning first, and then turn to local action.

6.1.1. Social Action, Social Planning, and Locality Development

Social action refers to the policy activities that a community's civic leaders engage in to influence the nature of life in the community. Their actions become prosocial when civic leaders define themselves and their interests as being shared with others in the community, and they shape their policies accordingly. Civic leaders who adopt a prosocial orientation expect to participate in the community. They utilize their positions and resources to initiate and support social actions that contribute to the community's quality of life and enrichment as a prosocial community. Further, social actions have a reciprocity effect on the other levels of development as civic leaders engage in programs and projects that contribute to changes at social planning and locality development levels.

Social planning activities are those carried out by professionals, administrators, and other qualified people who, in their societally intermediate positions of responsibility, apply their expertise within the community's laws and regulations to (a) influence civic leaders to develop prosocial policies, (b) develop plans and programs to implement policies, and (c) carry out activities such as teaching, counseling, and providing housing to serve the needs of people in the community. When, because of their professional skills and perspectives, these change agents define themselves as separate from the rest of the community and become focused on protecting and advancing their own status, they stop functioning in a prosocial way. However, when they define themselves as part of the community and apply their skills in ways that advance the quality of life in the community, they contribute to its prosocial development.

Locality Development is the term for the organized activities of members of a community who join together as individuals in a shared effort to address common problems. For example, individuals in a devalued, non culture-defining group (NCDG) may be excluded from educational and employment opportunities or their housing choices may be restricted to areas with inadequate housing and city services. When they join together to try to resolve the problems that they face because of their marginalization, they are engaging in locality development.

It is difficult to keep these levels of activity separate as they are intertwined in most ongoing enterprises. Individuals involved in social change activities may function primarily at one of these levels, but also try to influence changes at other levels. For example, school teachers (whose primary role is at the level of social planning) not only work out ways to organize and implement the curriculum (social planning), they may try to influence the community's educational policies (social action), and also participate with students in formal and informal activities to make their education more meaningful and enjoyable (locality development). The following paragraphs provide a number of research studies and programs that illustrate the ways these levels of action are ignored, implemented, or interrelated. They also show how those differences influence the effectiveness of those studies and programs. For example, in a program in Munich, Germany, children were organized to do research and make recommendations about providing opportunities to play safely in their neighborhood. Their participation was successful and valued at the community level, but often devalued and rebuffed by city officials (Stark, 1992).

Studies of the development of individual morality have yielded findings that point to the crucial importance of locality development in the formation of prosocial communities. Krebs and Denton (2005) recently reviewed Kohlberg's (1969) classic cognitive-developmental model of morality. His model emphasizes the invariant evolution of ever more abstract principles of moral reasoning as people's cognitive capacities develop. For example, infants are guided by Level One morality, responding only to discipline. Morally-developed adults respond to questions of morality at Level Five, with abstract reasoning that leads to making choices by evaluating, for example, the relative right to property versus the right to life. Further, Kohlberg's model assumes that each person's moral decisions will usually be made on the basis of the highest level of moral reasoning that person has achieved. That is, Kohlberg believed that adults will not make moral decisions based on different levels of moral reasoning in different situations, even though doing so might change their situation or their personal lives substantially in positive ways.

Krebs and Denton's (2005) more pragmatic model includes attention to people's affective considerations (their feelings, motives, and purposes) as well as their cognitions in making moral judgments. They summarized the basis of this framework as: "people make moral judgments and engage in moral behaviors to induce themselves and others to uphold systems of cooperative exchange that help them achieve their goals and advance their interests" (p. 629). Krebs and Denton's extensive research demonstrated that abstract reasoning, as conceptualized in Kohlberg's approach, has only a low level of relationship with morality-based choices. Instead, they found that peoples' real-life moral choices were more closely related to their personal involvement and consequences of their choices than to their achieved level of moral reasoning.

Whether moral choices are considered to be based on cognition alone or some combination of cognitive and affective factors, both views share a major primary premise. Their advocates agree that the basis for developing morality is cooperation and the maintenance of social networks. As Krebs and Denton's (2005) research supports, people are attuned to and motivated by their understanding that cooperation is essential to their own well-being. People experience conflicts between maximizing their own self-interests and strengthening their social networks, although in the long run, focusing on the latter strengthens those networks and also advances their own personal interests.

People at all stages of moral maturity use moral judgments in a variety of ways, including justifying immoral selfishness to advance their own interests. The belief that people at more advanced stages of moral maturity necessarily make less-biased moral judgments is not supported by Kreb's and Denton's research. However, even though people vary in their emphasis on and voluntary adherence to moral standards and their need for external correctives, it is the maintenance of a basic commitment to cooperation that better serves the interests of all involved. As Krebs and Denton emphasize, "if practiced by everyone, the ideal forms of reciprocity upheld by high-stage moral judgments are better equipped than more concrete forms to foster the interest of those who make them" (2005, p. 643).

Along with Kohlberg, Krebs and Denton believe that it is important for people to understand the function of morality. That is, morality serves to ensure that people "reap greater benefits by cooperating than by behaving immorally" (2005, p. 646). They concluded their argument by saying that exhortation or the teaching of moral principles (social planning) alone are not reliable means of creating moral societies. Rather, that task is more likely to be accomplished by organizing societies in ways that encourage individuals to gain greater benefits by behaving morally. Krebs and Denton, in essence, support locality development involvement as for the formation of prosocial communities. They see moral behavior as being crucial to providing a desirable quality of life for people and for providing a framework that will sustain and enrich them and their communities.

Lave and Wenger (1991) emphasized the centrality of locality development in the education of future generations as a prosocial community oriented undertaking. They developed a model of participatory learning from the historical practice of apprenticeship and argued that instead of formal education, it is the model for all learning. Their goal was to shift the focus of learning from viewing the individual as a recipient of outside wisdom to that of a participant in the social practice that maintains human civilization. To Lave and Wenger, all learning is situated in a context of practice. For example, apprentices, children, and others are "legitimate peripheral participants"(LPPs) in that they are both learners and contributors to society. They are also involved in a process of challenging and transforming locality development in that they question ongoing practices and are engaged in a struggle with their mentors, teachers, and others as they begin to eventually replace those "old timers" in society.

Apprenticeships constitute a kind of LPP, particularly in high skill level and knowledge acquisition (e.g., medicine, law, the arts, etc.). These advanced levels of education require institutions which are built and sustained by prosocial actions at the social planning and social action levels, but the learning processes within them are apprenticeships in locality development form. They vary in their combination of formal and informal learning, but overall they challenge the notion that learning is simply reproducing "task performances in routine ways" (Lave & Wenger, 1991, p. 65). Instead, "in shaping the relation of masters to apprentices, the issue of conferring legitimacy is more important than the issue of providing teaching" (p. 92). The point is that there is really very little direct teaching; much more common is bearing witness to the growing knowledge and capabilities the apprentices acquire. The learning process involves the apprentice in developing a view of the whole enterprise and what s/he needs to learn. The learning takes place through improvised practice as opportunities for it arise.

"Participation in the cultural practice in which any knowledge exists is an epistemological principle of learning. The social structure of this practice, its power relations, and its conditions for legitimacy define possibilities for learning (i.e., for legitimate peripheral participation)" (Lave & Wenger, 1991, p. 98). Learning does not occur by replicating the performance of others; it occurs through peripheral participation in the learning curriculum which exists largely as part of the ongoing developmental cycles of that community. We are all functioning at different levels of peripherality all of the time as we move from one activity or community to another. This is all part of an ongoing process of life and transformation from one generation to the next as we all participate in ongoing communities of practice.

Lave and Wenger concluded that, by decentering learning from being the preparatory activity of an isolated individual, "the *person* has been correspondingly transformed into a practitioner, a newcomer becoming an old-timer, whose changing knowledge, skill, and discourse are part of a developing identity–in short, a member of a community of practice" (1991, p. 122). This process has been followed for countless generations, even before more formal educational practices were established, and presumably will continue. Practice communities, so constituted, became prosocial communities and their citizens become prosocially oriented practitioners in the community. They can now contribute to the community as full members and begin anew the process of engaging future apprentices in peripheral learning and contributing to locality development, social planning, and social action throughout their lives.

In contrast and by ignoring locality development and social planning considerations, there is in the U. S. an ongoing effort to change our educational policies. Weinstein, a community oriented clinical psychologist, has focused her career on the study and improvement of school systems in the United States. Her work and that of her colleagues (Weinstein, Gregory, & Strambler, 2004) led them to conclude that the U. S. school systems cannot be reformed piecemeal. Rather, the national system's entire ecology needs reformulation. The localized school systems in the U. S. have an expressed goal of providing equal opportunity to all students; however, they are organized within an ecology that emphasizes selection according to merit and ranking according to achievement. Little or no possibility for equal opportunity is provided. To correct that disconnect, social planners will have to reconstitute the ecology so that it is based on access for everyone and their development as worthy individuals (Weinstein, 2002; Weinstein, Gregory, & Strambler, 2004). That is, although she does not use the term prosocial communities, she argues that school systems must incorporate everyone within their realm and involve them in creating a prosocial educational community.

This current disconnect has been imposed by the No Child Left Behind Act (2001). It is focused on achieving equality of educational outcomes by raising subject matter standards and instituting a standardized testing program to close the average achievement gap between children who differ by gender, class, race, ethnicity, and disability. The Act is based on planning and implementation approaches whose underlying assumption is that all children who enter the school system are equally prepared to benefit from a standardized curriculum. This assumption is simply not true.

In reality, U. S. children enter their schools with vast differences in their backgrounds, preparation and readiness for school learning, and personal styles of learning. They come from cultural backgrounds that foster different views of school and ways of learning. They are enrolled in schools with gross differences in the resources available to them and the quality of teachers who work with them. Further, this Act limits its definition of educational achievement to a narrow focus on three disciplines – reading, arithmetic, and science – and utilizes the single criterion of standardized test performances. For example, social studies, art, physical education, and other potentially creative endeavors such as manual and technical skills that might promote peaceful expression of diversity are ignored. Rather than providing positive support plus adequate additional resources and assistance to children and schools whose performance is below expected standards, these schools are faced with negative rejection responses. They are faced with the mandated threat of being closed if their students do not show continued improvement and fail to graduate. That is:

> These elements intensify a sorting achievement culture, likely to magnify negative self-fulfilling prophecies – the wrong expectancy equation. From segregation to resegregation to exclusion, there is still far to go in terms of putting in place a school culture that seriously develops the talent of a diverse population of children. Those wielding policy will judge positive expectations as unfulfilled rather than as narrow expectations never enabled. (Weinstein et al., 2004, p. 516)

The approach in the No Child Left Behind Act (2001) magnifies the effect of the cultural and socioeconomic inequities present in the current educational ecology by mandating social action policies that constrict school personnel. If the social planners had taken these considerations into account, they could have implemented social action policies that would have provided for prosocial benefits. Such social actions could facilitate prosocial changes at the social planning and locality development levels. Those levels are where teachers work and children try to learn how to value and respect themselves and their community while acquiring prosocial skills for improving their lives and contributing to their communities.

Instead, the Act produces negative effects by ignoring differences among children, arbitrarily raising standards, and restricting achievement measures to a select few educational areas. The responsibility for achieving the desired results is then placed on the shoulders of the professional staffs in the schools and the students who must meet these goals or be punished. Far from creating an ecology of acceptance, nurturance, and talent development in ways that include the children of the entire society and provides for the range of talents it needs, this approach further divides the society and blames its victims. Perhaps most contradictory of all its facets, it excludes the government, the central source of nationwide social action, from needing to change and be accountable for its unidirectional control over its proposals rather than being excluded from them. The No Child Left Behind Act is perhaps the most blatant and clear example of the importance and need for coordinating social action level policy changes with prosocial planning and locality development activities in conjunction.

Another example of how contexts influence peoples' interpretations of actions is embedded in Shinn and Perkins' (1999) findings about the different approaches and effects of work done by organizational and community psychologists to create system changes. They highlighted the difference between the two fields, pointing out that organizational psychology tends to concentrate on production, efficiency, and profitability of organizations. That is, organizational psychologists emphasize making changes at the social action and social planning levels to obtain greater production at the locality development level. Conversely, community psychologists focus more on the empowerment and well-being of individuals, particularly the disenfranchised. They concentrate on stimulating locality development to influence social planning and social action changes in order to improve the quality of life of disadvantaged community members. Shinn and Perkins urged both organizational and community psychologists to concern themselves with people's well-being *and* with their productivity so that organizations and people along with their communities will not only survive, but also thrive. The implications from their work and Sarason's (1972) include that social planners and implementers must consider all of these characteristics and concerns as essential components of successful change efforts. They must plan and implement change in an integrated fashion at all three levels; it does not work to change at one or two levels and expect to create overall system or community change.

Both organizational and community psychology seem to take as a given that communities and work organizations consist of adversarial groups. However, as just noted, organizational psychologists focus on changes from the top down.

They are more likely to approach change by working with an organization's leaders to change policies and practices. In contrast, community psychologists more often focus on changes from the bottom up by working with and for the less powerful and often marginalized segments of a community. Even so, when organizational psychologists focus on interfaces between different kinds of constituencies as in public or human service organizations, they too have to involve all of the different groups with their diverse and often conflicting perspectives and priorities. They then have to focus on facilitating ways to find common purpose across all three action levels.

Kotter and Haskett (1992) emphasized that point and called organizations that were able to satisfy customers, employees, and stockholders *adaptive cultures*. They found them to be more successful than those which did not satisfy all three of these constituencies. Such organizations were effective at creating prosocial communities in which the three levels of constituencies benefitted without exploiting each other. Kotter and Haskett's analysis highlighted the implication that community psychologists are well advised to consider integrating social planning and social action activities with the individual level changes they introduce. To successfully increase the effectiveness of communities and enhance their quality of life and that of the people in them, the entire community must be taken into account. Otherwise, change efforts may increase polarization or conflict rather than bring a community together for everyone's mutual benefit.

As mentioned in earlier chapters, Sarason (1972) has been involved throughout his career in efforts both to create alternative settings as vehicles of social change and in critiquing reasons why such efforts so often fail. He related these more prominent shortcomings to leaving the people and their contexts out of the plans for change, right from their initiation. That is, the planners and implementers did not take into consideration the history of the existing setting, the existing societal arrangements and values of the setting, or the people involved in and affected by the proposed changes. He pointed out that change agents often enter social settings with utopian assumptions. Among these are the beliefs that (a) their new approach will solve all of the setting's relevant problems, (b) the context will not change, and (c) everyone in the setting will have to change except the planners and implementers. Basically, Sarason emphasized that the seeds of failure exist in the characteristics and expectations of the change agents and of the contexts in which they try to create their utopias. He also emphasized that any endeavor to create community change is doomed to fail unless conflicts and the need to respond to changes in circumstances are acknowledged and addressed in an ongoing fashion.

6.1.2. Prosocial Community Processes

At this juncture, we can return again to the basic questions I have been asking throughout this book. They include: What changes are needed in our current approaches to establish a participatory approach to working with the ongoing psychosocial issues that arise in our individual lives and our communities?

That is, what do we need to do to integrate our efforts so that our social action, social planning, and locality development actions facilitate each other?

The primary answer to both questions is that broad, integrated changes are needed. Those changes need to be reciprocal and address both the nested frameworks of how we organize our societies and communities and how we organize our conceptions of ourselves as individuals and in relation to those around us. Specifically, in our predominantly individually-oriented Western societies, we emphasize our individual separateness from our communities, not our reciprocal relationships to them. Our societies also represent our locality development activities, social planning, and social action roles as being independent of each other and primarily adversarial. Consequently, the interfacing ethnic validity and psychosocial competence configurations that characterize individuals in the U. S. and in similar societies are not conducive to the formation of prosocial communities.

Lecturing about the need for changes will not lead to making them happen because the problems are in large part built into the nested framework that created them. For example, the social planning approach that needs to be changed in the health-related social and behavioral fields is the practice of reducing people's psychological difficulties to defects in those individuals and addressing them piecemeal. Complementary to that view is the belief that professionals can facilitate change processes without acknowledging their self interest in them or becoming involved in the actual change process itself. Parallel misconceptions also characterize the perspectives of civic leaders who formulate and manage social action policies. To create prosocial communities, all of us have to learn that our purposes can be better served if we reconceptualize how we understand ourselves and our communities. Instead of viewing each separately, we must integrate both as interrelated factors in a mutually enriching or diminishing interchange. It is in our individual and common interest to create prosocially organized societal arrangements. Doing so is an essential companion facet to the creation of prosocially oriented ways to behave as individuals.

On the contextual side of these interactions, we are all peripheral as well as primary participants in society, in our lives, and in the lives of others, including those we seek to serve because of their psychological dysfunction. We are all also mentors, although we seldom acknowledge the complexity of our participation. To create prosocial orientations in ourselves and our communities requires that we build a framework of joint individual and community prosocial commitment along with prosocial institutional structures and practices. That effort involves major changes in ways that we have not imagined, beginning at the level of our individual patterns of psychosocial functioning. Included in that process is the necessity of addressing and reducing what Bazerman (2002) calls the "omission bias" of people who believe that "they are completely moral if they obey a list of prohibitions while otherwise pursuing their narrow self interest" (p. 5). It is particularly important for those of us who are professional change agents to overcome that bias by redefining our work as part of life and society, instead of as being separate from it. Our codes of ethics and morality also need reformulation so that they support prosocial conduct. We also must become a part of the process of change and integration at all three action levels.

As communities emerge and become more complex, they also collect specialized knowledge and skills that not everyone can acquire. It would not be beneficial if everyone did try to acquire them. It is in the interests of the community's well-being to support selected community members for specialized training in return for their services. In this fashion, communities have developed many kinds of specialty fields and created arrangements to ensure that they serve the interests of the community and everyone in it. When the community's members function in the broader community's interests, locality development, social planning, and social action activities are carried out in a way that establishes and maintains a prosocial community.

We have no reason to believe that our lives as individuals and as members of our societies will ever be free of the tensions that arise when we face choosing between our individual rights to pursue our own interests and our concerns about the rights of others and the well-being of our communities. The latter concern involves taking the responsibility to engage in individual and collective activities to secure and advance the resulting shared benefits. We need to establish and maintain balances between the considerations that will create viable social arrangements and a rich quality of life for ourselves, others, and the societies in which we live. By contributing at the three levels of action to construct prosocially oriented institutions and ethical codes as well as to facilitate the development of prosocially oriented behaviors, we will, indeed, be contributing to the establishment of prosocial communities.

6.2. Creating Prosocial Communities

Prosocially oriented considerations and approaches become relevant when an individual or individuals set out to improve the lives of other people, particularly those marginalized within a community context. There is no formula or "cookie cutter" approach, structure, or predetermined outcome. It is counterproductive to begin such a task with the assumption that there is some theoretical conception of how a community *should* be organized. It is even more unwise to imagine that such a theoretical concept can be successfully imposed by self-appointed change agents within or outside of a community. Rather, each endeavor to create a prosocial orientation must be unique and must grow out of the people and their context. Unless the people participate as active agents (locality development), neither their perspectives nor their understanding of their community will be included in any of the changes that get made. Instead, the changes will reflect what the change agent wants. That outcome means the work will probably fail.

Community projects are usually organized to address one specific problem such as juvenile delinquency, bullying in schools, or inadequate affordable housing. It is often assumed that such problems can be solved in isolation. That is, the problems are believed to be the fault of those directly involved, i.e., the bully, the juvenile delinquent, or the people who cannot pay more for housing. The presumed answer is to focus on changing those considered to be at fault. The rest of the community is viewed as neither a contributor to the problem nor is it seen as needing to change in any way to address the problem. This way of defining a community problem and its presumed answer is actually part of what created that problem in the first place. Change agents have a responsibility to challenge that approach by introducing a prosocial community orientation. They can then become a partner with the community as they all work to change the interlocked conditions and ways people have been responding. The change agents and the community are then also likely to begin to see positive changes.

A prosocial community approach considers problems to be, in part, a function of the entire setting. Solutions are proposed, and then they are analyzed in relation to the community's ongoing dynamics to determine whether they are relevant for these particular people in this particular setting, and whether they can be constructively implemented. To resolve such problems, all of the participants, even those who are blamed for creating the problem, must be involved. Then the community can work together to resolve personal, relationship, and system difficulties that are contributing to the identified problem. Otherwise, community members will individually and collectively perpetuate their problems.

6.2.1. Assumptions Related to Prosocial Communities

Three decades ago, the assumptions held by most U. S. psychologists and other change agents reflected an individualistic/separateness set of professional beliefs about people and societies. They included that individuals in need are characterized by deficits, professionals are possessed with strengths and resources, and the solution to the problems of the needy is to provide professionally directed programs to assist them in overcoming their deficiencies or protect them from further deterioration or exploitation. Sarason and his colleagues (1972, 1979) disagreed and identified characteristics that they considered central to the success of their community development efforts (see discussion in Chapter Five). Those characteristics were based on a set of assumptions that varied substantially from the previously existing ones. The contrasting, prosocial community assumptions that emerged included that *resources are always limited* and *everyone has resources as well as needs*. Those assumptions led to a consequent third one, namely, *all can best be served by forming resource networks which are, of necessity, somewhat fluid and constantly being modified*. These modifications reflect the changes created by community leaders, professional and nonprofessional change agents, and other community development participants. Central to the development and nurturance of resource exchange relationships is the participation of resource network coordinators, i.e., individuals with particular sensitivity to networking opportunities and skilled at arranging mutually beneficial exchanges. These ideas can be stated as a fourth assumption: *leader-innovators who become involved as participant-conceptualizers are vital to successfully guide these kinds of program development.*

Following Sarason's (1972, 1979) lead, I came to believe that a comprehensive conception of prosocial communities and their development was needed. This conception rests on the definition of a prosocial community. Specifically, *a prosocial community is one in which everyone cares about others and the community as well as themselves, and consequently behaves in ways that will provide for the well-being of all and to the sustaining of that community.* The community's development rests on its members proceeding within the framework of a number of additional basic assumptions. They include that *everyone has a primary duty to maintain the community* so that it can provide a unifying prosocial network in which they can live and grow with a sense of well-being.

There are also assumptions relevant to the community as an entity. *Communities have a designated scope of concern and responsibility for maintaining and improving their well-being.* However, *they bear a responsibility to maintain collaborative prosocial relationships with adjacent communities.* For example, communities that use up *all* of the greater area's resources without regard to the needs of neighboring communities, will create major problems for their own citizens in the long run. Further, communities are complex in nature, and *they must accord equal respect to the diversity of their members, their unique ways of organizing their lives and their contexts, and their unique needs and resources.*

Kagitcibasi (1996) worked with her colleagues to develop a project to improve the situation of the residents, particularly the women and children, in a working class neighborhood of a city in Turkey. Their objective was to stimulate social development in that neighborhood through a program that combined changing individual and social characteristics. She believed that the level of social development in Turkey was low because of conservative family values, low levels of urban women's employment, and general lack of public support for early stimulation in children's development and preparation for school readiness. Kagitcibasi's goal was to retain traditional family values and emphasis on relatedness while encouraging autonomy in child rearing. That is, she wanted to change the nested frameworks and ethnic validity patterns of these families.

Kagitcibasi (1996) and her colleagues organized, implemented, and evaluated an Early Childhood Care and Education (ECCE) Program focused on educational, custodial, and home care development. All of the mothers' training was provided using a group dynamics format. The mothers were supported and encouraged to become involved as active participants. They were provided cognitive training including literacy, helped to develop more effective communication skills with their children, and were sensitized to the needs of growing children. At the six year follow-up assessment, the overall prosocial impact of the program was clear. Gains included not only cognitive and social development, but also enriched relationships between parents and their children. The mothers and children had higher levels of well-being as reflected in higher levels of self-esteem, improved social adjustment, and greater autonomy for the children. Kagitcibasi also found that the mothers had achieved higher levels of intrafamily status in their relationships with their husbands; consequently, there were now better spousal relationships between the parents. Further, there were higher levels of convergence between the parents and their children, who had become adolescents at the time of the follow-up. Note that all of these changes came without a diminution of family values and relatedness. In fact, the opposite had occurred.

The influence of the implicit psychosocial competence and ethnic validity assumptions underlying this project became evident. Kagitcibasi (1996) emphasized that this project was undertaken in a society whose people's orientations to themselves and others are separateness-relatedness rather than individualistic-collectivistic. To her, the latter is a psychological characterization, while the former is a societal one. I would differ from her view and describe both patterns as psychosocial. In either case, it has generally been assumed that there is an inevitable conflict between individualistic/separateness and community/collectivistic interests because these two perspectives support and discourage somewhat different ethnic validity patterns. Kagitcibasi argued that it is easier to create a prosocial kind of amalgam that integrates both perspectives in a culture that is originally relatedness-oriented than one that is separateness or individualistic oriented.

Whether we agree or disagree with her conclusion, it is important to note that constructive psychosocial spirals of development were successfully initiated in Kagitcibasi's project. Although it was not so conceptualized, this program created a more prosocially oriented approach to family and community development and demonstrated the importance of a transcultural conception of ethnic validity. That is, Kagitcibasi articulated the idea of combining separateness and relatedness in an Ethnic Validity Model, i.e., it combined the separateness characterizing Western societies and the relatedness characteristic of collectivist societies. She also implemented a program that provided families and their children with a way to embody their relatedness and separateness within their active agentry in a resource enhancing, prosocial way. In doing so, she demonstrated the value of a fifth prosocial community core assumption, *the change agent must begin by assuming a context is needed in which it is ethnically valid to behave in a prosocial way.*

Sarason and Lorentz described an important, successful project, the Bay Shore Resource Network. It was established by two community women who were involved citizen volunteers (locality development). Their goal was to establish a citizen participation resource network to improve "the mesh between the *needs* of citizens and local agencies and the *resources* inherent in both" (Sarason & Lorentz, 1979, p. 202). Emphasizing that needs and resources existed in both the citizens and the agencies, they successfully facilitated the establishment of a parenting education group run by trained parent volunteers and built a network of community parents who served as a resource group. Those involved found the idea of identifying reciprocal needs and resources of both the parents and the school to be a valuable, nonconfrontational way of addressing their perceived needs. As their activities grew, it became evident that at least two, full-time, neutral, community-based resource coordinators were needed. Their positions and the funding were arranged so that they were located in the interface between the agencies and the citizen groups (social action). Thus they were obligated to neither constituency and began the evolution of a prosocial community that effectively merged its informal and formal aspects in a successful and productive prosocial spiral of development (social planning). That is, they demonstrated their awareness of another basic assumption of a prosocial community: *A prosocial community rests on integrating the need for flexibility with the need for organizational stability.*

To effectively use a prosocial community oriented approach, we must first explore our own assumptions and their implications. These include the assumptions that we make about the contexts themselves (*prosocial communities*), the individuals (*psychosocial competence*), and the relationships between individuals and their context (*ethnic validity*). All of these assumptions are embedded within the broad nested frameworks that structure, contain, and shape the course of the lives of people and their communities, including you, me, and where we live.

I discussed the basic assumptions about prosocial communities in the above paragraphs. The following paragraphs spell out the related basic assumptions about ourselves and others. That is, they focus on whether (a) we have the capability of acting on our own behalf, and (b) we grant to everyone else that they, too, can be active human agents on the behalf of themselves and others. These two questions are crucial, and they must be answered honestly and openly.

A relevant analysis of how people's beliefs about their natures influence their behavior has been provided by Molden and Dweck (2006). For example, people who interpret behavior as indicative of trait or entity characteristics respond quite differently from those who interpret behavior as reflective of a person's status in an ongoing, process oriented trajectory. That is, people who think that the poor (or others who are marginalized) are intellectually and morally defective, do not expect them to change and so dismiss them. Those who think the poor are just trapped in a bad situation, expect them to change when given an opportunity. Consequently, change agents with the latter beliefs concentrate on using change processes in their work and expect people they are working with to respond accordingly.

Molden and Dweck (2006) also make the point that people are likely to use their different perspectives as guides for forming their larger systems of meaning and belief throughout their lives and when forming relationships at many levels. More specifically, if we view ourselves as acting on the basis of our human agency, but view those in a community with whom we are working as being limited by their trait-like natures, we will not treat them as agents like ourselves. Further, we will not enlist them as collaborators in creating change in their personal or community circumstances. In other words, to create prosocial communities we have to begin by first assuming that *everyone has a capacity of human agency*, that is, the capability for making judgments. Therefore, everyone is responsible for his/her own behavior as guided by an individual prosocial sense of morality (a conscience). That assumption includes that, like us, the people with whom we are working have a sense of human agency.

To be consistent in our approach, *we need to apply this reasoning in a similar way to the meaning and status that we assign to human dignity - as an attribute to which we are all equally entitled. Each of us with a capacity for human agency has freedom within the limits of respect for the equal freedoms of others and the obligation to sustain the community.* This second assumption leads to a third one because it makes it clear that *we need to approach our sense of morality as being both a product of our histories and experiences and of our sense of agency.* As just noted, Krebs and Denton (2005) documented that we all are influenced by our own perspectives and pertinent interests when making moral decisions. They also emphasized that for each of us, our sense of morality arises out of a sense of ourselves in relation to society. Although we may consider others to be functioning at what we consider to be a lower level of morality, we need to define our own conduct and theirs with the expectation that both their and our current perspectives are outgrowths of our histories and situations. It follows then that we can identify a fourth prosocial community assumption. That is, *we are all capable of changing in both prosocial and antisocial ways.* Only when we can see ourselves as citizens participating in our own lives and activities are we able to attribute the same to those with whom we work to create changes. From these four assumptions, we can begin to build a personal psychosocial competence foundation for developing a prosocial community approach.

The relationships between ourselves and others (who serve as outside influences in our lives) is what I refer to as our self-world relationships. These self-world relationship perspectives are also an integral part of our psychosocial competence characteristics. The nature and meaning of these aspects of our lives and interactions range from our individually unique attributes to those of the more inclusive groupings of which we are members. They range from our friendships and families to ever more abstract levels all the way to and including our national and cultural memberships and affiliations. In a most fundamental way, they include our senses of our rights as individuals along with our duties to others. As we consider the nature of our self-other relationships, we encounter the relevance of another assumption, one about the nature of prosocial justice. That is, a prosocial conception of justice rests on the assumption that *justice processes will be open and fair to those involved and disputes will be resolved in an open and fair prosocial manner with an emphasis placed on correcting injustices in ways that to the extent possible restore damages done and preserve or strengthen the community.*

Self-other relationship assumptions apply to hierarchical as well as equal-status and both informal and formal interactions. For example, broadly evident culture defining group/non-culture defining group (CDG-NCDG) status differences and expectations weigh heavily in considerations of how we establish formal and informal relationship expectations and patterns of interaction such as the development of mutual trust or willingness to be self-disclosing. We begin to build an orientation for creating prosocial interactions to the extent that we (a) see our interactions and relationships as process oriented and potentially emerging, and (b) see everyone as equally subject to these same processes and in need of learning from each other. Such interactions will be particularly influenced by our capability to view ourselves and others as interacting citizens and also as experts with regard to each of our own particular experiences and roles.

When we act on these prosocial community assumptions, we begin a process of psychosocial leaps and spirals (Tyler, F. B., 2001). That is, we make a psychosocial leap whenever we make any choice about how to see ourselves, others, or the world, or approach them differently. No observation, thought, or desire in and of itself compels us to act or believe differently. Rather, we proceed by an act of agency to formulate a new interpretation or understanding, and then behave accordingly. Once we make such a leap, whether it involves deciding that we like someone or that this is our community, we start to act on that liking or sense of belonging to build a more encompassing friendship or a more active role in enjoying and enriching our community. Although we are often unaware of the impact of such small decisions or changes, over time they can lead to profound shifts in our senses of ourselves, others, the world around us, and in the ways we approach and address the events in our lives. At other times we experience these leaps as profound insights or world-shaking revelations, such as when we fall in love or become disillusioned with our country or our religion. In either case, these changes can variously begin progressive, constructive spirals of growth and maturity or destructive spirals of dysfunction and dissolution. Further, these patterns of psychosocial leaps and spirals characterize the prosocial development or non social destruction of our families, communities, and societies just as they do of ourselves. We try to facilitate these kinds of psychosocial leaps and spirals when we seek to build prosocial communities in order to solve what we previously had thought of as isolated problems in a few people or a particular neighborhood in our community.

Similarly, our experiences in benign, predictable, and supportive situations and environments influence us to make the leap of organizing and pursuing our lives in an active, organized, and planned fashion. By contrast, in environments that are unpredictable, hostile, and threatening, we often make a leap to expectations of unpredictability, including erratic and predominantly mixed threats and punishments from others. We begin to acquire a defensive, opportunistic, and frequently self-destructive cycle of behaving. We, or other change agents, who want to counter such negative approaches to life have to model positive prosocial behavior. We must also provide threatened and insecure individuals with opportunities and support for beginning to make positive prosocial leaps. We can be effective only if our most basic assumptions about ourselves and others allow us to assume a prosocial perspective.

When there is a resource enhancing relationship between people's psychosocial competence characteristics and those of their sociocultural contexts, we speak of that psychosocial competence configuration as being ethnically valid. When their sociocultural contexts are transcultural, we speak of their adaptive psychosocial competence configurations as being transculturally ethnically valid. The context may be benign, predictable, and supportive, or it may be malicious, unpredictable, and destructive; all contexts present different demands and possibilities. Consequently, the first assumption regarding ethnic validity is that *the way to become ethnically valid is to acquire a view of oneself and the world, and of how to build on that relationship in a way that is congruent with the new situation's characteristics*. That process is essentially the same in any context.

When anyone who has developed a productive, ethnically valid style in a specific context enters a new and different context, his/her habitual approach is legitimately considered not to be ethnically valid in the new situation. To reconcile that disparity so that the person can thrive and the context can be enriched by this new person's participation, either the person or the context or both must change. Thus, the ethnic validity prosocial community assumption is that *both the requirements of situations and what is ethnically valid in them can change.* People and situations are flexible. Both are able to accommodate to the new expectations that are introduced when new people enter an ongoing situation, and communities can and do change in response to people and their requirements upon entering and leaving.

I hypothesized and confirmed among CDG high school and college students in the United States and India (Tyler, F. B., Dhawan, & Sinha, 1988) that competent high school and college youth who have been socialized in a predictable, benign, and supportive environment that fosters active agency would have relatively high scores on internality, trust, and active planfulness. We also found that the NCDG youth patterns differed from those of the CDG students in both contexts, particularly on internality and trust variables. Recent studies by M. E. Aguilar-Agafie (Personal communication, July, 2005) who also uses these measures found that more competent college students in a hierarchical, authoritarian religious college in Teheran, Iran, and one in Lebanon were external and passive but high on trust. That is, for those students it is ethnically valid in their hierarchical, authoritarian context to make the psychosocial leap to become passive, trusting of those in authority, and externally directed.

6.2.2. Comments

A long time ago, I (Tyler, F. B., 1973) argued that people who are excluded from a community have little choice but to define themselves in opposition to that community, a hypothesis that has been verified in numerous studies with street youth and other marginalized youth. The converse has proven equally valid. That is, when rejected and marginalized youth are provided benign support and opportunities to make psychosocial leaps to more prosocial ways of life, a preponderance of them do so (Tyler, F. B., 2001). That is, they learn a new psychosocial competence configuration that is ethnically valid in their new life context. To reiterate, the approaches that prove effective in facilitating prosocially directed leaps are the ones that change the possibilities in people's situations. That is, we create a different context, one for which a prosocial psychosocial competence configuration will be ethnically valid, model the desired behavior, and treat the involved individuals accordingly. That approach provides people a pathway to follow so they can adapt to and even contribute to building a prosocial community environment.

There are certainly other projects and programs that incorporate parts of the prosocial community ideas and activities that have been included here. After all, prosocial community development is not a new idea. What these examples provide is a framework and illustrations that can be used in an approach to the construction of prosocial communities. What I have added is an empirically supported conception of the matrix of our lives as a nested framework within which we construct individual psychosocial competence configurations that interface with those networks in an ethnic validity fashion.

After exploring many programs and studies to find a constructive approach that reconciles our needs and desires for both individuality and connectedness, I encountered this quote from the writings of Confucius:

> When the Grand Harmony was pursued, a public and common spirit ruled all under the sky. They chose men of talent and ability, whose words were sincere, and they cultivated harmony. Men did not love only their own parents, or nurture only their own children. The elderly were cared for till the end of their life . . . Provisions were made for widows, orphans, childless men, and the disabled. . . . Possessions were used, but not hoarded for selfish reasons. Work was encouraged, but not for selfish advantage. In this way, selfish schemings were repressed. Robbers, thieves, rebels, and traitors had no place, and hence the outer doors remained open, and were not shut. That was what we called the Grand Harmony. (Hua, 2005, p. 62).

Our present day prosocial community ideas are implicit in what Confucius imagined millennia ago. I am not writing to advocate such a utopia nor am I even imagining one. Rather, in concluding this chapter, I return to where I began the book. Although forming prosocial communities will not solve all of our problems, unless we form enough of them to sustain our societies, our societies cannot sustain themselves. We cannot create prosocial communities unless we specifically focus on doing so. That we can do so successfully is described in the following final chapter. It documents a comprehensive, successful, and ongoing prosocial community oriented program that continues to expand and is now becoming part of the society of an entire country. We can start in small settings as they did or with large complex ones, and build and sustain more mutually satisfying and enriching ways to share our common existence. Finally, we can invite our children to participate with us, and then we will know that they are living in warm, loving communities.

7 Questscope: A Comprehensive Prosocial Community Program

This chapter was written in collaboration with Dr. Curtis N. Rhodes, Jr. President and International Director, Questscope, Amman, Jordan (see biographical sketch, P.145) Chapter Seven describes in substantial detail the origins, development, evolution, and ongoing nature of a strong prosocial community program, Questscope for Social Development in the MidEast (hereafter referred to as Questscope). It is a comprehensive, non-governmental organization (NGO) whose programmatic activities are located primarily in the Hashemite Kingdom of Jordan, a predominantly Muslim country. Questscope started its outreach program to provide a better life for marginalized youth and their families in the MidEast. It now has international roots with charters in Great Britain and the United States and the support of the Jordanian government. Its work is also supported by international agencies such as the World Bank, the European Union, and individuals from Western and MidEast countries. It is included here as an exemplar because it effectively integrates all three action levels of prosocial communities.

7.1. History and Evolution of Questscope as a Prosocial Community

Dr. Curtis Rhodes, Jr., Questscope's General Director, is a United States citizen with a background in public health. He went to the MidEast in the early 1980s as a faculty member at the American University of Beirut. Caught up in the turmoil in that region, he changed his focus in order to contribute more directly to the well-being of the citizens of Lebanon, Jordan, Palestine, and Syria. In 1988, he consolidated his interests by organizing support for and then establishing Questscope. The organization's expressed mandate is to "Putting the Last, First" (Questscope, 2006). It provides disadvantaged communities with program assistance for the most defenseless members in ways that better serve their vital role in their community. That is, "the capabilities of neighborhoods and local institutions are strengthened so that they take an active role in improving the lives and experiences of those most vulnerable in their communities. Everyone then becomes an active player to make things better for one and all" (Questscope, 2006). The basic goal is to engage the entire community in that effort.

By 1997, Questscope had developed a variety of unrelated, ongoing programs to improve the lives of underserved youth and women in Jordan. Dr. Rhodes had begun searching for a conceptual framework to organize those disparate projects into a common, comprehensive development strategy. He believed that combined mutually beneficial programs could then contribute more effectively to the progressive improvement in the lives of those they served, as well as their communities and larger societal contexts. In a broader sense, Dr. Rhodes was seeking a framework to enrich Jordan's communities by incorporating the most vulnerable marginalized members, street youth and their families, so they could contribute to changing the conditions that perpetuated their marginalization.

I gave an invited address at the 1997 United Nations Urban Childhood Conference in Trondheim, Norway, entitled "Urban Settings, Youth Violence, and Prosocial Communities" (Tyler, F. B., 1997). Dr. Rhodes was in the audience and subsequently contacted me to explore the possibility of adopting a prosocial communities framework for his organization. He persuaded my wife (also my professional collaborator) and me to serve as his external program evaluators as he began to organize Questscope's activities within that framework. We made an initial onsite evaluation in 2002, and have continued to work with him and his staff as consultant advisors. During this time the creative and far-reaching elaboration of the prosocial community (PRSC) approach by Dr. Rhodes and his colleagues has been instrumental in the success, expansion, and impact of Questscope's programs.

At this point each of Questscope's uniquely focused programs and projects has been adapted to a PRSC model and embedded in a collaborative, overarching PRSC consortium. In order to manage and continue developing within a PRSC framework while it continues its rapid growth, Questscope has become a complex, multi-layered organization.

7.1.1. Levels of Change

To guide change in human relationships, patterns have to be established that everyone involved will use. As explained throughout this book, the PRSC model emphasizes three central elements, *Locality Development*, *Social Planning,* and *Social Action.* Each element must be developed in relation to the others for a program to be effective. Alone, each approach is limited and often ends up in conflict with the others, but when they are combined they complement each other. When Dr. Rhodes began to work with this framework, the emphasis on linking those three elements together as equally active contributors struck him as a vital addition to his existing approaches. The information that was presented about PRSC frameworks in the earlier chapters is integrated with Questscope's activities in the following paragraphs.

Locality Development. Locality Development was defined earlier as coordinated approaches that look for convergences among people and groups and then use them as a basis for working together. Within Questscope, the focus of Locality Development is on building a consensus among neighborhood members as they seek to identify issues and develop plans that will enable them to work collaboratively in addressing those issues. When the people in a neighborhood focus on common concerns, they are motivated to come together. Their convergence stimulates them to undertake collective actions that lead to desired changes. The people in these neighborhoods have the capacity to identify their issues, set priorities for action, and manage resources to bring about positive change in cooperation with children and youth, if they are assisted in collaborative ways as partners. "Children and youth from disadvantaged communities deserve the opportunity to become citizens in a society that desires their inclusion and involvement" (Rhodes, 1998, p. 32).

This process involves stimulating those in a specified neighborhood to change their customary ways of functioning and begin to adopt new approaches. It also requires the professional community to adopt new roles as facilitators and learners. Fortunately for interested change agents, there is a body of knowledge available that provides guidance for introducing and disseminating such innovations. Rogers (1995) pointed out that this approach follows a relatively universal S-shaped trajectory whether it concerns social changes in informal and formal community, public and private health, educational, or business and manufacturing organizations. That trajectory is characterized by gradual increments of use by participants. It begins with those who have had a broader range of experiences, are more widely informed, and are more open to exploration and new experiences. Subsequently, there is a rapid spread of change followed by a final slow increase until nearly full utilization is achieved.

These same strategies are used at Questscope. That is, Questscope staff help to initiate the process of locality development by building on the voluntary participation of marginalized segments of every community in which they work. As local development activities are increasingly engaged in and joined by larger segments of a community, a greater need is created for professional assistance to accomplish their objectives.

Social Planning. We learned previously that Social Planning involves local experts and service-providing institutions working collaboratively with the community to solve problems the community has identified. To contribute to the building of prosocial communities, experts have to redefine their roles and tailor them to match a community's identified needs, rather than using their professional paradigms to diagnose the community and its members to impose solutions that are valid only in those alien paradigms. In a World Bank Institute report about providing better lives for street children, Volpi (2002) pointed out that the issues confronting any marginalized individuals or groups require more than good intentions. They need professional expertise and assistance for their amelioration. They also require integrated, multifaceted efforts to reach the children where they are, enlist their participation, provide them with individualized attention, involve their families and communities and, when appropriate, reintegrate them into their families, schools, and labor markets. In addition, professional expertise is needed to provide essential services and to lobby for the children's well-being and for creating a more benign social environment.

To address these requirements, Questscope put its program's focus on the needs of the marginalized and on networking with formal and informal agencies to provide appropriate access to assistance and to sustain successful efforts. Questscope does not begin tasks with a specific focus and a designated termination date. Instead, it begins with a vision that will bring those who are peripheral towards the center and mainstream the marginalized as important players in their lives and in their societies. Each of Questscope's endeavors is tailored to the people for whom it is designed, to their circumstances, and to their expressed needs. Questscope has created and guided the development of its prosocial community processes by continuous use of feedback from regular evaluations to redirect its efforts toward meeting the changing needs identified by project participants. Providing problem-solving feedback to the community's positive actions leads the participants to take even more positive actions, and thus a prosocial spiral of development builds.

As a general example, a community's trouble with disruptive youth may lead to excluding them from its programs. PRSC oriented personnel can help modify that problem with their collaborative community approach. They can help to assess the youths' circumstances, identify their grievances, and work out ways for community members to see themselves through the youths' eyes. Then the community members, the professionals, and the troubled youth can work together to find ways for those youth to become constructive participants. Over time, the collaborative maintenance of these kinds of supportive conditions reduces the destructiveness of the youth, as they become participants in the community. This kind of solution works for everyone's benefit.

Social Action. Social Action was defined in Chapter Two as official and unofficial actions by civic leaders to change the policies and circumstances in a community in ways that affect the lives of the residents. Questscope staff work with their community project participants to bring about beneficial social actions for marginalized children and their families by bringing their situation to the attention of civic leaders in appropriate ways. Those leaders can then eliminate or modify conditions that create hardships; they can make changes that instead provide possibilities. Questscope's approach to Social Action is to stimulate paradigm shifts. When leaders make such a shift, they begin to define marginalized communities as being worthy of inclusion. Next, Questscope guides civic leaders to develop their skills of listening to the marginalized and other community members, and then cooperating with all of them to better meet everyone's needs. This approach requires that civic leaders shift from conventional views of their roles and status to seeing themselves as fellow participants in the community.

7.2. Program Development Process

7.2.1. Forming a Community

As Questscope began to adapt its approach to one of developing prosocial communities, it became clear that there is an essential, trans-ethnic validity process, i.e., stages of growth, that every group of people must go through to become a genuine community (Peck, 1988; Tyler, F. B., 2001). Those steps or stages make it clear that developing a prosocial community, as with developing any community, is an ongoing process that is valid across all cultures, although the process manifests itself in different ways according to cultural expression. It begins with a superficial pretense of similarity, marked by conflict avoidance and the denial of individual differences, e.g., hiding and ignoring differences. Culture-defining group (CDG) persons function well at this level. Eventually, individual differences come to light and people in the group try to eliminate or obliterate them by identifying and addressing or fixing the problems in others. CDG persons will attempt to keep the upper hand, but non culture-defining group (NCDG) persons will cause discomfort and dissension. To resolve the conflict, each person in the group must consider what part he/she is bringing to the problem. They all begin to explore the issues that need to be addressed and resolved, including: expectations and preconceptions; prejudices; ideology; the need to heal, convert, fix, and solve; and the need to control. Finally, people must deal with their vulnerabilities, try to resolve their shared concerns, and invest in developing a prosocial community. While these steps may, at times, seem formulaic, it is important to understand that no community is sustainable unless there is constant renewal of these learning cycles. Communities must invest and reinvest in continuing their renewal process within a prosocial community framework.

7.2.2. Roles and Relationships

There are many essential participants in every community site (Hardister, 1985). Each person or group has a different part to play and multiple role relationships. Not everyone has the same role, but all roles are valuable; indeed, if we discount some roles (like "the opponent") then we risk sabotage by the person who has been left out. The other major roles in community development projects are defined below.

A *legitimizer* is an individual, group, or agency that confers credibility on, in the case of community development, an organization or program. Obtaining legitimacy is necessary for the organization to be respected and accepted and for its programs to be effective. For example, Dr. Hamdi Murad is an influential, respected Islamic theologian and governmental leader in Jordan. He agreed to work with Questscope by lending his support to ideas regarding poverty and children (especially girls), helping to legitimize its community programs designed for young women.

A *target group* is made up of the individuals for whose benefit the development intervention is undertaken. The target group is identified by demography (those who live in a particular place), or characteristics (those in poverty, subjected to violence, or are school drop outs), or by any other way that can be used to identify a specific population group for whom a service or intervention is intended. It is important to distinguish the target group from the *beneficiaries*, who are a subset of the target group. *Beneficiaries* are those who are actually recipients of a particular program or service offered by the organization. An organization may mistake its beneficiaries as being representative of the target group, leading them to generalize and replicate program interventions that have been effective with those beneficiaries even though they are not typical of the larger target group. Such mistakes often result in failure of the program. It is important to solicit feedback from non-participants in a program (i.e., those who are in the target group but not among the *beneficiaries*) in order to fully understand the impact of the program on the community. Questscope's target group for *Non-Formal Education* is approximately 80,000 to 100,000 children between the ages of 6 and 16 who have dropped out of Jordan's formal school system. The current beneficiary group, actual participants in the Non-Formal Education program, numbers 200–300 children.

The *Partners* are community organizations who collaborate with Questscope to achieve mutually agreed upon objectives. Ideally, the Partners will eventually be able to assume long-term leadership roles for and direction of those objectives, i.e., their program. Questscope has participated in establishing its mentoring program in a number of Partner organizations such as the government's Juvenile Correctional Facility.

Advocates are individuals or groups who support and participate in planning and developing an organization's cause or program. Several referral organizations in Jordan such as the Higher Council for Youth work with Questscope's mentoring program to provide youth with additional services and access to activities.

Individuals or groups who challenge the work of an organization in a community become *Opponents*. Although opposition may be destructive at times, it may also have positive outcomes. For example, it may cause the organization to address or clarify faults or inadequate parts of its original program.

Colleagues are professional individuals or groups who may offer specialized knowledge, information, experiences, contacts, or skills to an organization's work in a community. Questscope works with large numbers of colleagues on a wide array of organizational activities. Colleagues may become *Partners*, but also have the potential to become *Opponents* who challenge Questscope's work if they are not interacted with appropriately.

Resources persons are individuals who do not have a particular interest in the actual development work of the organization, but who are helpful in supplying information, materials, funding, access to resources, etc. They may be important societal leaders such as Dr. Hamdi Murad, the Director of the Ministry of Islamic Charities.

A *Regulator* is any person, such as a member of a government regulatory agency, who ensures that the organization complies with laws and regulations in the community. If treated properly and with respect, regulators may be of assistance to the work of the organization rather than bureaucratic obstructionists. The policy and management personnel in the government agencies in which Questscope has Partner arrangements are necessarily Regulators.

7.3. Questscope's Program Elements

Questscope is a complex organization. It is important to understand the nature of its elements because each of them plays an important role. Further, the fitting together of these elements in a complementary and supplementary way is essential to the successful continuation of the organization and the accomplishment of its prosocial goals. Those elements, the Administrative, Collaborative, and Programmatic Structures, are discussed in the following sections.

7.3.1. Administrative Structures

Questscope has a *Board of Directors* in the United Kingdom and one in the United States, plus an *International Council* of advisors. It also has *Executive Staff* offices in the United Kingdom, the United States, and Jordan. To fulfill their responsibilities, staff members must be appropriately qualified to perform their job responsibilities. However, from a PRSC perspective, that is not enough. Even the people working in parts of the organization at the furthest distance from direct contact with the marginalized youth and their families must be able to relate them and their perspectives. That is, everyone's views, staff and community, are included throughout the organization. Questscope can then work collaboratively and with reciprocity to resolve how the respective components of the organization are to function.

In practice, this requirement does not mean that every office can include disadvantaged youth or their parents. It does mean that those who assume program roles must be socialized in on-the-ground experiences and perspectives by at least having some personal contact with community members in relevant settings. In Dr. Rhodes' terms, all personnel must undergo paradigm shifts in perspective. They must come to see themselves as part of the community process. Consequently, everyone needs to be informed and evaluated by everyone else. No one can stay protected from challenge. After all, the only way to gain the trust of marginalized people and their communities is to be as open to them as you, the outsider, expects them, on the basis of your presumed good intentions, to be open to you. That is, outsiders, even those far removed from the disadvantaged groups' needs, must demonstrate that they can understand the groups' needs first hand, and ensure them that no one will be neglected or slighted. Community members must feel that they and their community's interests will be given first priority, even at the central levels of policy and administration.

Questscope also has administrative structures at its program and project levels ranging from its central directorship to projects located in specific neighborhoods. They all must meet the paradigm shift requirement of developing a constituent-centered perspective. The specific nature of those jobs and involvements are discussed later in this chapter.

7.3.2. Collaborative Structures

A crucial aspect of Questscope's programs is that they are all collaborative. Programs are never undertaken unless a government, community, or local organization requests Questscope's involvement and agrees to work with its collaborative approach. For example, the current mentoring programs in Jordan are based on a broad agreement between Questscope, the Ministry of Social Development, and the Department of Public Security of Jordan. The Ministry of Social Development participates through the Juvenile Correctional System, the Directorate of Public Security through its Family Protection Unit and Anti-Drugs Unit. These agencies are not only Partners, they also serve as legitimizers and regulators. This cooperative relationship is seen by Jordan's government as part of its comprehensive, national development process with a civil society model for government-non-governmental organization interrelationships. Questscope has grown because its institutional leaders and program participants have become engaged in listening to each other to better inform the practices of each. Pilot projects are established to create visibility. They provide occasions for everyone to listen to what is happening, learn what the basic problems and resources are, and begin to respond in an informed and collaborative fashion.

At the level of specific projects, a variety of people and agencies are necessary participants. There is a *home institution*, that is, a specific organization (e. g., a neighborhood social service center, a religious institution such as a mosque) that asks for and adopts or otherwise commits to undertaking a Partnership Program. Questscope participates in the Partnership by learning about the institution while socializing it so that it can adopt a PRSC approach. This institutional capacity-building process takes place as a result of teaching the Partner's staff how to establish and carry out Questscope's *mentoring program* which is described in greater detail later in this chapter. It is focused on meeting the needs of disadvantaged youth, age 10–22. *Mentors* are volunteers recruited from the local community and trained to serve as role models and friends for the youth. *Case Managers* are counselors or social workers employed by the home institution to select and train *Mentors*. They also oversee and coordinate activities in the program. *The local community*, ranging from the families of mentored children and youth to neighbors to local businesses and organizations, helps by providing education, jobs, and financial help. In fact, children's families or guardians must sign consent forms and agree to participate before their children can be included in the program. *Referral organizations* such as local or national institutions provide services (employment, legal, health, sports, etc.) when the mentoring program links the children to them. Because many of the underprivileged youth have to work to support themselves and/or their families, participation by organizations that facilitate job opportunities and training for better jobs in the future is invaluable.

7.3.3. Programmatic Structures

7.3.3.1. The Mentoring Program

As indicated above, mentoring programs are the central part of Questscope's approach to youth. They are the core mechanism around which local action activities are organized. The mentoring programs are designed to provide a holistic approach for meeting the emotional, cognitive, social, and economic needs of at-risk youth. They enable mentors to establish meaningful personal relationships with adolescents by involving them and collaborating with them in prosocially oriented activities. Efforts are made by mentors to engage the children in activities that will increase their influence on their circumstances, give them opportunities to assume responsibility, and emphasize mutual cooperation.

The mentoring programs in Jordan target primarily marginalized male street youth and isolated young women. They were developed after Questscope's initial work with young, at risk males. These programs have necessarily been modified to provide more appropriate help for young women as their social circumstances are quite restrictive. Major elements of these mentoring programs are outlined below.

Through the mentoring process the mentor has the opportunity to identify the child's concern, problems, ambitions, and needs. The child and the mentor work together in prioritizing and setting relationship goals. Each plan includes one goal, which is achieved through four weekly activities. Each activity has a set date, time, objective, and description of the tools to be used. Both the child and the mentor work together in implementing activities and in setting new monthly goals.

Throughout the mentoring relationship, the child is assured of access to assistance from a wide variety of service providers or referral organizations. These institutions also participate in capacity-building with Questscope to help them better serve at-risk children. At present, referral institutions include the Higher Council for Youth, the Vocational Training Corporation, University of Jordan Counseling Department, three charitable associations that specialized in micro enterprise projects, the Family Protection and Anti-Narcotic Directorates of the Department of Public Security, three sports clubs, and the Al-Hussein Center for Performing Arts.

Boys. Activities for these adolescent boys are focused on enabling them to function and develop as active citizens in the world outside of their homes. Arabic masculinity symbolizes independence. It is thus acceptable for men to have problems or make mistakes that may require correction, and/or rehabilitation without the seriousness of retribution that females face. Male youth require mentors that may be a few years older than they and a little further ahead in their development to provide role models for them.

One-to-one activities are central to mentoring with a focus on the needs or interests of the child. They may simply involve letting the youth decide where to go for a snack. They may also be more extensive and involved, like agreeing to spend a week with the youth at a Wilderness Camping Program, a Referral program provided by the Jordanian Army Special Forces. *Group activities* involve mentors and youth going as a group on recreational outings or engaging in educational activities, such as going to a soccer game, a nature program, or a picnic.

Supporting activities include a range of functions. The first, *Street education,* is the part of the *In-Formal Education* program which teaches children that learning to read and write and acquire other relevant skills is enjoyable, valuable, and possible. *Group economic projects* include creating or engaging with small group businesses that can provide a safe working environment in which young people can earn money while developing skills. *Community service projects* provide youth an opportunity to contribute to their communities. They also enable the community to see the youth as prosocially engaged. *Drama activities* provide positive ways for youth to express themselves and understand their own tensions through writing and acting out their struggles. Children have written and performed plays dramatizing their problems. Some of these plays have been videotaped and distributed for public education. *Sports activities* such as forming teams and playing soccer provide positive activities for self-expression and a chance to work together while following rules. *Group counseling* provides a forum for a trained adult to talk with (not to) groups of children about their problems and the issues they face in their lives. Their issues range in severity and include concerns about personal doubts, self-defense, and lack of social skills needed to handle educational and employment challenges.

Girls. Major programmatic elements of the mentoring program have been adapted for young women. These changes are sensitive to traditional culture and include looking to the past for validation and to give meaning to the present (Giddens, 1990). Arab society is a specific example of a modernizing culture in which the consensus regarding how to build an environment of trust is changing. Consequently, those who work with young females must be sensitive to the strong influence of traditional culture in Arab society.

Traditionally, Arab females also have had a symbolic role; their actions (most significantly their mistakes and problems) reflect not simply on themselves, but on their family and tribe as well. Therefore, instead of a girl being seen as having a problem, she is often considered to *be* the problem. Females are not granted room to make mistakes or to have problems so they live under the rule that there is no problem because there can't be a problem. The result is individual self-censorship on the part of young women and social group-censorship by everyone else around them to avoid violating their symbolic status and bringing about shame.

Young women, especially those with low socioeconomic status, are often socially isolated within a restrictive environment to protect their honor and that of the family. This traditional view means that any approach to help them improve their lives must take place within acceptable limits. Girls and young women, especially those at risk of abuse or neglect, need activities and experiences that will help them form a positive self identity and better prosocial skills while also reducing the social isolation in which they live. Since a female has a very visible symbolic role in society, changes to be made in her life require the support of the whole community. In other words, for women's programs to be acceptable, they must be considered legitimate by the community.

Questscope accepted this perspective and sought legitimization through religious leaders before establishing a mentoring program with young women in the community of Zarqa (a suburb of Amman). Questscope approached the Zakat Fund within the Ministry of Islamic Charities and asked its director, Dr. Hamdi Murad, to speak in the local mosque every Friday for one month. Dr. Murad covered the topic of poverty, with special emphasis on young males and females, to enforce a social atmosphere characterized by the notion that good Muslims care about helping boys and girls in poverty. By suggesting that girls could bring benefits to their struggling, low-income families if they were permitted to receive some training, Dr. Murad provided the community with a new and reasonable social context for understanding solutions to the problems facing females.

The success of this effort demonstrated the remarkable potential for improvement of the lives of Arab girls and young women when that improvement is supported within cultural boundaries. Such changes always have a wider impact than expected, if brought about with support from legitimizers. That is, if community and religious groups indicate support for an idea or program and deem it respectable, parents are likely to follow the trend and give their support, just as happened in Zarqa.

Respected female religious teachers were the only outsiders for whom it was culturally acceptable to visit homes in the conservative area of Zarqa. These teachers from the Ministry of Awqaf volunteered to visit low-income girls along with female Questscope staff and invite them to join Questscope's program. Since the mosque is the only place that many young women are allowed to go outside of their home, the program earned massive, high profile respectability by holding all activities there. Once they began coming to the mosque, young women developed what were often their first meaningful relationships with any females outside of their homes. Previously isolated young women were able to discuss their problems, make friends, and discover and develop their own interests and aspirations. Because the girls' project at the mosque began with cooking classes, they were able to develop a skill that enabled them to be more helpful with their families' responsibilities. Simultaneously, group mentoring took place, so girls also had the opportunity to converse with and learn from Mentors.

There are additional program elements that were adapted for the young women. Questscope recruited women who had previously had greater support in their own lives for taking on more autonomous roles to be mentors and case managers. Consequently, they were more self-confident and socially engaged and could share and model those attributes. The mentors who were chosen were adult women who understood the life passages of young Arab women and were able to be role models. Unlike male mentors, requirements included that they had to be considerably older, have raised children, and be in good standing in the community. As older women, their reputations would not be affected by associating with younger women who were uneducated and from low-income families. While female mentors often came from contexts and backgrounds similar to those of the girls, they also must have had exemplary life outcomes and become established in their respective communities within culturally respected roles for women. These carefully chosen requirements allow Mentors to have a self-directed role and exert positive influence as change agents. The mentoring experience also promoted the personal growth of the mentors.

Questscope's approach has many implications for working with women of a NCDG status, including that it engenders positive change from within the system rather than attempting to change the culture from the outside. The approach and mentality is not to fix problems of society, but to foster growth within society. If people are allowed to develop and grow as human beings within their society, they will inevitably bring about positive changes while still maintaining cultural distinctiveness. Prosocial changes can then be incorporated as the culture develops resilience as a key to cultural survival. Cultures can be remarkably flexible, especially when there is no threat to their integrity.

The women's activities and projects parallel those of the boys. They were, as noted, adapted to the girls' distinctive needs and the restrictions on their lives. For example, their educational activities include learning about personal hygiene, reproductive health, and more general topics such as the benefits of a healthy diet and regular exercise. Their *Group Economic Projects* include working with small businesses that could provide a safe working environment in which young women earn money while developing skills. For example, newly created businesses for young women have included livestock trading, marketing mobile phone accessories, and becoming beauty consultants. Some of their activities have even provided them with socially sanctioned interactions with boys. In one program, girls and boys formed a "shadow government" for their city. In *Drama Activities,* girls are provided positive ways to express themselves and their unique problems, often together with boys. Such program activities allow young women to deal with issues of social interaction, friendships, solving conflicts, their emerging creativity, and other topics they might not otherwise have the opportunity to face or discuss.

Education as a central aspect of mentoring. Early on, Questscope began using educational interventions as a component and extension of its Mentoring activities. It implemented *The Earn and Learn Program* based on the observation that many young boys were working and not attending school. If they did not bring in certain amounts of income for the family each day, they often faced serious consequences such as not being allowed to eat or sleep inside. Mentoring created a kind of apprenticeship program for children in which they worked and earned money for half a day, learning more about their job and developing additional skills with the guidance provided by economic mentors. The other half day was devoted to teaching the children to read and write, with the eventual option to return to the educational mainstream. The Earn and Learn Program was eventually expanded to a *Street Education* program. Currently, it has been developed further as a *Non-Formal Education* program, in which participating children begin with street education and progress to a certificate from the national Formal Education system.

Street Education and *In-Formal Education* programs are characterized as *"Short Cycle" Learning.* Children are taught something abstract, and then it is immediately made concrete to create a permanent connection and recognition. For example, children could tell you exactly where they go in the city at night by making a simple sketch, but they could not relate their sketched map to the actual map of the city. Questscope developed a liaison with the Civil Aviation Authority to fly children over the city so they can see that the paper map is simply a different representation of how the city was laid out. Another example is from the literacy component. To help themselves learn to read, children wrote their own readers or texts based on their own life stories (as opposed to reading a generic Dick and Jane story to which they could not relate).

Questscope's goal in street or in-formal education is to make learning fun and get children excited enough about it that they become interested in returning to a formal educational process. Street children have little or no concept of delayed gratification because they live in a world where, when they find an opportunity, they must take advantage of it immediately or someone else will. As a result, when it comes to education (which requires delayed gratification), they have no incentive to wait for a benefit delayed into the future. Therefore, by making In-Formal Education fun, children learn that long term benefits will come even while they also enjoy an immediate benefit, i.e., fun while learning.

In-Formal Education classes require at least one trained facilitator who may be a volunteer and is not necessarily a teacher. In fact, this "street educator" may even be a street kid who is simply further along in the learning cycle. The keys to instruction in this program are face-to-face interaction and dialogue between the facilitators and the children, so that children can become the leaders of the learning process.

The methodology practiced by In-Formal Education has been codified as *Participatory Educational Methodology (PEM)*. As a teaching methodology, it can be incorporated in teacher training and improvement. An informal "certificate" recognizes the child's achievements at this "entry" level and encourages the child to continue. It is an important tool for celebrating and rewarding the child's small victories, although it has no official status.

Non-Formal Education (NFE). These programs were developed from the experiences gained while working with children in the In-Formal Education program. The purpose is to work with children who have dropped out of school so that they may have access to tenth grade certification and further technical and vocational educational opportunities. In Jordan, if children drop out of formal school for more than two years, they are not allowed to reenter the formal system. Most do not have the option of pursuing home study because they must work.

The NFE program is a way for children to continue their education and keep their jobs. The NFE program is divided into three levels, each eight months long, each covering a variety of subjects including Arabic language, Islamic culture, mathematics, social studies, vocational training, and life skills. They attend classes for two years, for two to three hours in the evenings, five days a week. Children may begin in either Level One (substitutes for grades one to four) or Two (grades five to seven), depending on the amount and success of their prior education. Upon completion of the third level (grades eight to ten), students must pass standardized tests created by the government especially for this program. If they are successful, they receive a certificate that is equivalent to completion of 10th grade. The official recognition of his/her achievements allows the child to continue to progress upward in society as he or she chooses.

Questscope and the Ministry of Education (MoE) recruit certified teachers to act as facilitators who prepare NFE students for tenth grade graduation. Extensive training manuals prepare teachers with the proper skills and background for this PEM approach so that they learn to interact in a new way with students. Retraining of teachers, many of whom have taught for over 20 years in formal schools, impacts not only their NFE students, but also their students in formal classrooms and their personal lives.

NFE aims not only to impart knowledge to students, but also to develop in them a critical consciousness that empowers them and allows them to see the reality of their experiences in a new way. Among other differences, children go from having a narrow and inflexible view of themselves to seeing themselves within the context of relationships and the social setting. They move away from quick judgments based on a shallow viewpoint, to being able to suspend immediate personal judgments. They also shift from allowing their personal priorities to drive their actions and relationships to comprehension of the rights and obligations of others.

The Vocational Training Corporation (VTC) is a government institution that trains students for certain technical jobs and careers. Children who graduate with certificates from NFE may attend VTC just as do students from formal schools. Although specially admitted as NFE students, upon graduation they receive exactly the same certificate as students who have previously attended formal schools. At this point, NFE students have been reintegrated with their peers in terms of formally verified qualifications.

The National Development and Employment Fund (NDEF) has formally agreed with Questscope to create mechanisms to provide for small business loans to students who successfully complete the VTC entrepreneurship course and want to start a business. The successful mainstreaming of street children and the erasing of the stigma of being an "at-risk street kid" is thus accomplished by graduating from VTC and obtaining a loan. The availability of these loans ensures that previously marginalized children are given chances from which they were formerly excluded.

The PRSC model has been applied to all components of Questscope's educational programs. At the community level, children are able to learn in a casual environment and become interested in more education. Local volunteers become involved by helping with street education of the children. Questscope also demonstrates to families, community members, and employers the value of having these youthful employees resume their educations. At the institutional level, linkages are maintained with the Ministry of Education whose staff design curricula, tests, and criteria for certification. Teachers in the formal system implement NFE classes, a practice which has introduced innovative methodology to the teaching profession. At the third level of the PRSC model, civic authorities in government departments become involved as they begin to understand the potential of educating dropouts and commit themselves to developing legal alternatives for the education of those students.

7.3.4. Program Implementation

7.3.4.1. The Structure of Program Implementation

Questscope's primary influence is as an outsider, an agent that brings the potential for change to each setting as it seeks to understand and address it. But because it uses a prosocial approach, Questscope must learn how, in each specific instance, to become part of the setting rather than remain apart from it. Consequently, even as Questscope leads and provides new information and structures, it engages in learning and being led.

The implications of this collaborative process include that the prosocial model for social change must extend across all of the levels of the social structures, including the policy making levels, the middle institutional and civic authorities, and the locality development groups at the bottom levels of the society. In other words, the Prosocial Community Model must be applied at all three levels to ensure long-term, sustainable change. Those who begin working with Questscope in any of its diverse activities are required to first engage in experiences with the Questscope collaborative prosocial approach. Only after they have demonstrated their commitment to and capability of interacting professionally and personally in this fashion are they brought into administrative roles.

7.3.4.2. Levels of Program Implementation

Overall, the direction of each Partnership is carried out by a *Questscope Program Director.* Providing guidance to program implementation at *the locality development* level includes helping to involve the child's family and neighbors plus local businesses and organizations. Their role is to support children and provide new possibilities for the participating youth through education, jobs, and financial help. An integral part of each Partnership project is engaging the family and neighbors in the prosocial process of introducing Mentoring and its related programs into the community. This process is considered the best way for the Partners to appreciate the benefits of Questscope's approach. Finally, local and national organizations serve as *Referral Organizations* that provide specialized help (e.g., legal help and health care) and opportunities (e.g., sports and job training). Most of the resource participants are themselves volunteers, underscoring the prosocial orientation that is essential for developing the core characteristic of these programs and their contribution to building a more prosocially oriented society.

At the Social Action/Social Planning *Institutional Level*, Questscope has a dual role as it is both a peer with other institutions and the officers of those institutions, and it is an external organization bringing new ideas into those institutions in its effort to build a prosocial community. It must cooperate at the social planning level along with the other institutions. Questscope cannot create a prosocial community as an outside director of the process, and it cannot exclude itself from the process it is trying to build. In that role, it may also arrange for providing relevant training for the program's home institution personnel. Trained counselors, social workers, and advanced psychology students serve as officers who coordinate and oversee activities that Questscope provides with Partners, including selecting and training Mentors.

At the 2002 Dead Sea Conference mentioned in an earlier chapter, the attending representatives had been previously unaware of each other's mandates and programs, and there had been no opportunity to show a willingness to cooperate on behalf of children. Because it was part of this process rather than detached from it, Questscope was able to stimulate the same kind of learning and understanding at this inter-organizational leadership level that it creates at the community level. A result of the conference was that, for instance, the El Hassan Youth Award (a non-governmental organization) and the Public Security Department (police) developed new ideas for cooperating in their approaches toward youth.

At the *Social Action Level* of interacting with civic leaders, Questscope brings the positive accomplishments to their attention and involves them. Questscope points out that such changes will, in turn, reflect positively on those civic authorities as well, a win-win situation. Questscope establishes prosocial ways of cooperating with these authorities without attributing blame or shame to them for earlier policies of ignoring or resisting prosocial development. This strategy makes such authorities generally willing to be responsive and cooperative about taking social actions when community problems need to be addressed.

Examples of civic action impacts stimulated by Questscope's program activities include that the Mayor of Amman waived the policy of requiring payment (key money) for using stalls in local markets so that young street youth entrepreneurs in Questscope projects can sell their goods there. Also, the Minister of Social Development terminated employees in a Juvenile Correctional Center when he was informed of their abuse of inmates. In addition, the Amman Municipality recently cooperated with Questscope in conducting a Participatory Rapid Appraisal (see following section) in four targeted areas of Amman. Following that appraisal, the Municipality made a commitment to provide additional funds to improve its ability to serve disadvantaged children in those areas. Such responses are a reflection of the civic authority's interest in being involved in the success of Questscope's prosocial programs.

7.3.4.3. Program Phases

The implementation of complex community programs is a daunting task when the goal is to improve perceived inequities and injustices. It requires understanding that specific steps must be taken to reach the goals of justice and equality. Achieving that objective requires planning the program carefully and working through a number of phases as outlined below. When an organization asks to form a Program Partnership, Questscope undertakes the task of determining the institutional capacity of the organization and its ability to sustain a program (mentoring or NFE, for example) long term.

Participatory Rapid Appraisal (PRA). Questscope uses the methodology of Participatory Rapid Appraisal (Chambers, 1993) to determine whether an applicant organization (a) has appropriate relationships with the target groups that will support a prosocial approach, and (b) is amenable to the formation of a Questscope style partnership to facilitate its ability to meet its defined needs and goals. Although the Questscope staff who conduct a PRA are doing so at a community organization's request, they do not use strict methods and rules with narrow-minded and sometimes leading questions to interview people. Instead, they approach the organization's members with attitudes and behaviors oriented to supporting the free expression of the new members' opinions, knowledge, and suggestions about the area. The Questscope interviewers structure this discussion in an open ended fashion to help the interviewees develop their own ideas about how to improve on their community's situation.

PRA involves behavioral innovation because it changes the behavior of both those conducting the PRA and the community organization's members. The PRA also provides community members with tools and skills they can use as they work with Questscope to structure and prioritize the information collected. One tool used to accomplish this is called "mind-mapping." Questscope staff write the various participants' ideas on paper to help connect and organize the diverse viewpoints of a wide variety of individuals in multiple roles. Mind-mapping captures ideas by brainstorming. It brings out ideas and images about community organization structures, interconnections, and steps needed to build toward feasible solutions for improving their situation.

PRA enables both the local organization and the community members to have the perspective and insight of outsiders so that they can see themselves functioning in their own system and see the changes they can make. Because they still remain insiders, they also have the ability to actually bring these new changes into existence. By making a choice to conduct the PRA, Questscope commits itself to helping both the local organization and the community with the problems that they identify. The result is a project, program, or activity designed by community members, with the help of Questscope as a new member of the community. This process also fosters prosocial relations between all of the participants.

Logical Framework Approach. This approach is an analytic method used by Questscope to assess whether planned or existing approaches will accomplish the Partner's identified objectives. It builds on the PRA results and serves as the basis for planning activities that are needed to implement Prosocial Programs for this new Partner. If it is determined that existing activities will not enable the Partner to reach its goals, the assessment shifts to determine whether adapting Questscope's procedures or adding others can effectively complement those already in place.

Cycles of Program Implementation (Illustrated in Application of the Mentoring Program). The program of each partnership is implemented in a sequential way to accomplish its immediate objectives. By the time the Partners' program is actually initiated, those involved have begun to create among themselves a more prosocially oriented community to help the target population and also sustain their prosocial community. Questscope also works toward incorporating the new Partner into a broader network of such communities who support each other and participate in extending the network to include even more communities. Thus, at the broadest level, Questscope activities are interrelated in ways that serve to change the society in which they are nested. These changed societies are less likely to create alienating patterns and more likely to continue building prosocial orientations among their citizens in the ways they organize themselves and use their resources.

At the specific level of implementation of each Partnership, the newly developed structures used to accomplish the program's objectives are incorporated into three cyclic stages. These activities take approximately five years. The stages are described here:

Cycle 1 involves Questscope and the new partner in implementing the chosen program, in this case a Prosocial Mentoring Program. As explained earlier, this one-to-one, Mentor-Mentee program is established as the center of a constellation of activities designed to include disadvantaged children in mainstream society. Potential Mentors and Mentees are recruited from the larger community, Mentors are trained, (one-to-one with Questscope staff) and the other support activities described earlier are developed. The emphasis during this cycle is on implementing these activities and building the Partner's capacity to assume future responsibility for this program. Questscope's primary task is to model effectiveness and professional standards to the Partner.

Cycle 2 is focused on capacity building and efficiency. Particular attention is given to the improvement of the Partner's management administration, especially in its use of resources and directing of its staff. The emphasis of Questscope shifts from modeling to overseeing the quality of ongoing activities. This new stance is central to the PRSC approach because this keeps everyone engaged in building the prosocial nature of themselves and the program. That engagement grows out of continued participation in creating and improving the holistic focus of the ongoing activities.

Cycle 3 ensures that the Partner can function autonomously while maintaining and building on its PRSC orientation. Questscope shifts to assuming a role as program facilitator. It may provide interim funds, grant writing assistance, and additional support staff to assist the Partner in becoming financially self-sufficient and self-governing. The Partner is kept engaged in the broader task of expanding its prosocial community focus by assuming representation on Questscope's National Steering Committee for at-risk children. That committee, in turn, provides the Partners with general guidance and support. The Steering Committee was formed as a continuing Partnership between Questscope and the Ministry of Social Development.

7.4. Facilitating Prosocial Transformations

Questscope assumed that the best way to address problems related to the rising numbers of marginalized urban children throughout Jordan was to offer to get involved in ways that would respond to situations that communities identified as troubling. They began with activities that involved collaboration with the children and their neighborhood communities. Questscope's rationale was that since children spend most of their lives in their communities, that is where they begin to form their approach to adult participation in society. The community teaches them how to conduct themselves and acquire the competencies to guide their social participation in ever widening circles. If children are to become significant contributors to improving their own lives and communities, they presumably need to learn how to identify their own needs and the types of remediation that will best serve them. Because the children's existing skills and competencies, antisocial and otherwise, have been acquired in their present context, they know how their environment needs to be changed to make it possible for them to be included in prosocial ways.

Questscope developed and uses several measures to evaluate the impact of its program interventions. It also uses these measures throughout Jordan to assess the nature of the contexts and situations of vulnerable youth and their families. The findings from their first major assessment of a Program's pilot phase were used to revise and implement additional program interventions. It also led to the construction of additional evaluation measures whose findings, in turn, were used to determine the direct effects of the expanded programs on the participants.

Enlisting the support of significant adult interaction was the beginning of the prosocial mentoring approach in one-to-one relationships with children. It grew from the idea that prior to the cognitive development and competency that accompanies later adolescence, children develop their sense of self based on the expectations of adults. That is, if adults believe in the potential of children, the children around them will rise to that potential.

In addition, this highly intensive and individually customized program could only be sustained at the community level with the support and involvement of other institutions. Civic authorities, including especially those working in the Juvenile Correctional System, were trained to take on central roles as Questscope Partners. Their organizations were then defined as mentoring institutions, and they took on responsibility for management of inter-institutional networks for referrals, delivery of service to children through volunteer mentors, and support and supervision of the relationship.

The emphasis throughout the three cycles involved in establishing a mentoring program with a Partner is on helping the Partner to build a governing and funding structure. Training within each cycle is approached as the formation of new perspectives on the basis of knowledge as well as guided practice. At the end of Cycle Three, the role of Questscope in institutional capacity building is completed. Completion of all three cycles can take up to five years.

The Central Figures. The *Mentees* are at-risk youth with backgrounds of poverty and/or broken families. They often have dropped out of school to work and help support themselves and their families. Some are in trouble with juvenile authorities, and some participate in anti-social behaviors such as substance abuse, violence, and other illegal activities.

Mentors are trained volunteers from the community, often students from universities. Since the university students are fulfilling community service requirements by providing community service, they gain both extrinsic as well as intrinsic satisfaction from their participation. The relationship is reciprocal and prosocial. After training, they become part of a pool from which the children select their personal Mentors. Granting the children the right to choose emphasizes their right to their own autonomy and control of their lives. The goal of mentorship is to establish trusting relationships with the children without adding any complications or restrictions. As their relationships with their Mentees grow, Mentors become new role models for how to behave or acquire new life goals.

The *Case Managers* are the only paid staff in the Mentoring Program and are supplied by the mentoring Partner institution. They supervise Mentor-Mentee relationships so that Mentors do not have unlimited and potentially destructive unaccountable influence over the children. They sustain the volunteer/mentor role by providing support to Mentors, and allowing the Mentor to do his/her job without taking on burdens or commitments that others such as referral organizations or professionals can manage. Depending on their abilities, each Case Manager may oversee up to 35 relationships. They talk to the children before the Mentoring relationship begins in order to learn about each child's background, priorities, interests, and goals. This conversation helps the Case Manager understand the child as a whole human being. During the Mentoring relationship, the Case Manager holds frequent debriefings with both Mentee and Mentor. This process provides insight to the Case Manager for discussions with the Mentors who, as volunteers, do not have the experience or mandate to act on many of the Mentee's serious issues, for example, medical or legal questions. The responsibility for taking such actions lies with the Case Manager. Finally, Case Managers arrange for periodic case conferences (at least one per child) so that all concerned parties will come together and consider actions that will best benefit the child. Thus, they also act as the liaisons between child, community, family, referral organizations and the partner institution.

The Process. The mentoring process begins with an initial evaluation to establish whether children are mentally ill or severely emotionally damaged. This assessment identifies the children for whom mentoring is not the appropriate intervention. Questscope then directs them to the proper organizations for the help they need.

Before beginning the Mentoring Program, the children are given a pre-test, an assessment based on questions from many domains, to establish a baseline for the nature of each child's situation and capabilities (Rhodes, Mihyar, Al-Bustami, & Al-Khouli, 2004). Next, the Mentor, Mentee, and Case Manager develop an individualized plan for each Mentee with goals and specific activities designed for reaching those goals. Every activity in every plan is strategically designed and thought through by the Case Manager and Mentor so that it contributes to the child's progress toward every goal.

Goals are directed at social and behavioral changes such as improved social skills, vocational maturity, realistic self-concept, cognitive abilities, and decision making. Examples of goal-related activities are getting ice cream, going to a museum, visiting a library, reading a book, talking about dreams and aspirations, and hiking and camping (usually a group activity). Prior to the mentoring relationship, the child may have only been in a store in order to steal. For that reason, shopping may be a selected activity. With the Mentor present, the child will (it is hoped) be treated as any other child with money to purchase something. The child then learns how a normal shopping experience feels. The Mentor has modeled a new kind of behavior in this situation, helping to create awareness of what it is like to belong to society. The impact of the experience and the role modeling thus can increase the child's desire for integration or reintegration.

The Mentor and Mentee meet three hours per week for (ideally) 12 months. At the end of this mentoring relationship, the children are given a post-test. By comparing the two sets of test results, the Case Manager will have a measure of the child's progress and the effectiveness of specific activities for meeting the child's goals.

Importance of Prosocial Mentoring. Applying the PRSC framework to the Mentoring Program created increasingly expanding activities and outcomes. At the community level, as the Mentor models new behaviors, the child begins to change. The Mentor is also impacted by the relationship, perhaps one of the most serendipitous and valuable spin offs of the Mentoring Program. This effect has already created in Jordan a cadre of at least a thousand socially-aware young people in their twenties who now use positive rather than rejectionist responses to such social issues as injustice or poverty. Case Managers bring the children's changed behaviors to the attention of parents and the greater community, encouraging both to provide the type of activities for children that will reinforce their new, positive behaviors and their positive upward growth spiral.

Such changes also begin to have an impact on the institutions that are involved with Questscope. The Partner institutions in which Questscope vests its Mentoring program remain responsible for organizing, sustaining, and supporting their own programs. They identify children in their catchment populations, recruit financial support, apply the mentoring process manuals, and maintain ethical and professional standards. Juvenile Correctional System centers and local NGOs are exposed to the PRSC framework which potentially influences their approaches. All types of institutions begin to develop new views of how they can serve the community, possibly through creating or improving access for the target group and others, maintaining accountability, and developing collaboration between all parties.

As mentioned earlier, Referral Institutions are those to which Questscope and/or partner organizations can send children for additional counseling, medical, dental, and other specialized help and opportunities. These organizations do not actually mentor the child, but contribute from their specialities to the mentoring relationship. However, their participation links them to both the individuals they help and to other participating organizations. For example, several sports clubs agreed to receive and involve children from the Juvenile Center in various athletic activities. The Higher Council for Youth, a referral organization, then made an agreement with the Ministry of Social Development to involve youth from the Juvenile Center, which it oversees, in the Higher Council's Youth Leadership Program. As Questscope Partners, representatives from both organizations attended The Dead Sea Conference which was a meeting of referral institutions. Discussions among these attendees led them to better understand the process and see ways they could improve their help for the children. Consequently, their participation led them to bring further changes to their own organizations.

Finally, civic authorities (as demonstrated by the Juvenile Correctional System) have been exposed to Questscope's alternative approach. Not only do they participate as Partners, they have adapted the approach for their own institutions. Because of its visible success at the community and organizational level, Questscope was invited to develop a mentoring program within Amman's Juvenile

Correctional System with funds provided by the World Bank. Civic authorities, especially those in the Juvenile Correctional System, are sometimes part of the problem, but they are also a necessary part of the means to solutions. These authorities must be influenced to change aspects of their organizations that are negative (e.g., fire people who abuse children in Juvenile Correctional facilities) and create positive new possibilities (e.g., provide rehabilitation options).

By working with the Juvenile Correctional System and police, Questscope is raising the community's consciousness that incarceration of children who offend (either by participating in antisocial or illegal activities) has undeniably negative effects on their development. Diverting the children from their antisocial behavior must begin at the point of police contact. Rehabilitation organizations must reform or redirect the roles of their present social workers, training them to become mediators who act on the child's behalf. Trained staff with roles similar to probation officers can provide rehabilitation and address the meaning behind the children's antisocial behavior. The goal is for children to be incarcerated only in exceptional cases of serious crimes.

In the near future, Questscope will train Amman Municipality's 100 staff members in such rehabilitation approaches, a result of the Municipality's involvement in PRAs in four areas of Amman. Questscope is also working with juvenile justice legal reform, currently under way in Jordan. The Ministry of Social Development has an agreement with Questscope to allocate a portion of its budget to the continuation of its Mentoring Programs. A manual of procedures for Juvenile Correctional Facilities was published in July, 2006, for application of the prosocial mentoring approach in all juvenile centers. Changes at this level of civic authority are what has made the long-term development of the Mentoring Program possible (Al Khouli, et al., 2006).

Mentoring figures based on the primary example of the Juvenile Correctional System provide an overall picture of the potential impact of this approach. Questscope's target group is approximately 12,000 children. Of these, 6,000 have characteristics of juvenile delinquency but have not yet been arrested, and 6,000 have experience in the juvenile system. Currently, the beneficiary group is approximately 3,000 children within the Juvenile System, including those in correctional/reform institutions and abandoned children (wards of the State).

Establishing Mentoring in Partner Programs. As described earlier, three cycles are involved in establishing a mentoring program in a Partner. Upon completion of Cycle Three, Questscope can withdraw from direct program involvement. In other words, training is not simply imparting knowledge and information to the Partner. It is also focused on guiding the Partner to becoming a self-sustaining prosocial community and a participant in a community of such programs. Questscope's emphasis in Cycle Three is on helping the Partner to build a governing and funding structure. For example, the goal for the Juvenile Correctional System is to have the Mentoring Program incorporated into its government budget and imbedded in its structure as a government organization. The goal would be the same for an NGO, but NGOs require assistance to build their funding base as Jordan, like most governments, does not currently provide funding options to NGOs for such programs.

As increasing numbers of organizations throughout Jordan become interested in implementing the mentoring program, Questscope will not have enough staff to conduct the mentoring cycles in its customary way. Thus Questscope and participating organizations will have to begin a cycle of change. For example, organizations wishing to incorporate the official Questscope Mentoring Program by using Questscope material and obtaining Questscope support will have to fulfill certain criteria. For example, they will need to have staff members available who are capable of carrying out the Case Manager role. Since the overall process of initiating new Mentoring programs is ongoing and progressive, accreditation of such programs is a future goal. Once that goal is reached, new Partner organizations will be expected to pass certain milestones to earn and maintain their accreditation. A team of individuals and groups will continue monitoring the progress of the new Partner organizations. Reproduction of the Mentoring Program in new Partner organizations will become a collaborative process incorporating a variety of formative training tools. Partner organizations will, for example, study the twelve Questscope manuals, watch Questscope DVDs, visit Partner organizations that are already conducting the mentoring program, and learn from referral organizations.

Mentoring Clubs. Mentoring Clubs already provide a network of resources, support, and activities so that experienced Mentors can continue to improve and remain ready for and interested in mentoring. These clubs study the latest films and books related to mentoring, listen to talks from former Mentors, and receive visits from former Mentees. They also serve as places for Questscope to train new Mentors and also teach trainers. These clubs are vested in universities throughout Jordan with university professors providing additional training and instruction on general volunteering and social work. Questscope has trained thousands of mentors, 400–600 of whom remain active. Because of the Mentoring Clubs, these volunteers stay ready to mentor thousands of young people. An added bonus is that the impact of Questscope's training program values remains with the Mentors, even if they do not continue in the program.

Prior to beginning the mentors' clubs, volunteers struggled with not having access to professional guidance and advice. The Ministry of Social Development (MoSD) also suffered without a link with the Mentors. For instance, in the juvenile detention centers, Saturdays were reserved for families to visit their children. However, Mentors would often create a conflict by also showing up to see the children on Saturday. In September, 2005, a Mentor's Camp at Ajloun Nature Reserve was held to address such issues; attending representatives were from the MoSD Mentors, and from a variety of different clubs. The goal of the camp's activities was to foster open communication and cooperation between the different mentors' clubs and between the clubs and the MoSD. Outcomes of the camp included three agreements: the MoSD agreed to provide the clubs with direct financial support and access to other funding agencies; the clubs made a commitment to continue training new volunteers and to develop partnerships and coordinate activities with local civic groups and the MoSD; and the Mentors clubs agreed to exchange studies and information regarding the program. The mentor clubs and these interagency agreements are additional examples of the intermingling prosocially oriented networks that have formed within this broader prosocial context. For example, the mentoring club members grow and develop within their local club, and the clubs get together on a regional basis to stimulate additional growth and development for each other.

7.4.1. Impact of Mentoring

When Prosocial Mentoring was initiated in 1998 with funding from the European Union and other European donors, a database of dependent and independent variables was established to provide for ongoing evaluation of the program's efforts. Questscope developed its mentoring as part of a prosocial community approach by creating project designs and implementations for emerging programs and in response to the inputs of children, volunteers, and partner organizations. In 2002, the World Bank Japan Social Development Fund underwrote the expansion of Prosocial Mentoring in the Juvenile Correctional System in order to better respond to the identified problems of disadvantaged children. Those problems included dropping out of school, underage employment, being in juvenile custody, and experiences of violence and abuse. The low income levels of the families were an underlying constraint that kept the parents and these children impoverished. Consequently, the identification of an effective holistic approach was required to reverse their social alienation and support their reintegration into mainstream social and economic opportunities.

Questscope's programmatic response was to build and evaluate a holistic community approach centered on a professionally guided mentoring relationship between the child and his/her mentor, where each one gets to know the other and identifies common interests, hobbies, and abilities. Steps in the development of Questscope's programs were evaluated periodically and modified to build on that feedback. In 2006 a comprehensive evaluation was completed (Al-Khouli, All-Zou'bi, Mihyar, & Rhodes, 2006). Questscope analyzed data from 310 children who had completed one month or more in a mentoring relationship (drawn from 968 children who participated in a wide variety of referral activities during 2000–2005). The purpose was to identify the effect of the mentoring program (jointly undertaken by Questscope and the Ministry of Social Development in Jordan) on personal competency and social integration among disadvantaged children. The children were 7 to 18 years old; 90% of them were between 13 and 18 years old. Ninety percent of the children were in juvenile correctional centers and the rest in care facilities for abandoned children who were wards of the State.

The assessment scales used in this evaluation included the Dean Scale (Dean, 1961), Heppner and Petersen's Problem Solving Scale (1982), The Al-Kilani and Abbas Self-Concept Scale (1980), and the Crites and Savickas Vocational Maturity Scale (1995). They were adapted to use with Arab children, and used to measure changes in four domains: social alienation/reintegration, problem-solving skills, self-concept, and vocational maturity. The variables in each scale are as follows:

The Dean Scale (1961) was used to measure social alienation. The scale represents measures in three dimensions: (a) feelings of inadequacy, (b) absence of values, and (c) social isolation.

Heppner and Petersen's Problem Solving Scale (1982), as adapted by Abdel Kader in 1983, was used for assessment in three dimensions: (a) self-confidence in solving and facing problems and making the right decisions, (b) ability to gather information and set forth effective solutions, and (c) self-control and the ability to manage one's emotional responses to problems.

The Al-Kilani and Abbas (1980) Self-Concept Scale was used with children ages 7 to 16 to measure self-concept in eight different dimensions: social value, self-confidence, mental ability, physical ability, general health, emotional stability, activity, and aggression.

Crites and Svickas Vocational Maturity Scale (1995) was used to assess vocational maturity. This scale measures two essential dimensions: children's tendency towards work and children's efficiency in making vocational decisions.

Each child was assessed twice: a pre-test at the beginning and a post-test at the conclusion of the mentoring relationship (Al-Khouli, et al., 2006). The relationship was initiated when a child chose his mentor, and weekly meetings between them were held for up to one year. Information used to prepare each monthly plan (four weekly activities) for the mentor and child came from a number of sources, including: A personal interview by a case manager, a case conference with the mentor, child and case manager, and the pre-test results. The study sample was divided into two groups: 150 children who implemented less than three monthly plans and 160 children who implemented three or more monthly plans.

Differences were found in all four domains between pre- and post-test results between the two groups. Multiple regression analysis also found that the number of monthly plans completed by each child and mentor had the greatest impact on all dependent variables in the study, including social alienation/reintegration, self-concept, vocational maturity, and problem-solving. Results from children who completed less than three monthly plans were significantly different from those who had completed three or more monthly plans (Al-Khouli, et al., 2006).

The results of this study are consistent with the conclusions that Grossman and Rhodes (2002) reached in that the impact of the mentoring relationship becomes stronger with time. They are also slightly different with regard to the length of time needed for the mentoring relationship to achieve the desired results. While Grossman and Rhodes concluded that the mentoring relationship might need a year or more to show change in various aspects of a child's personal development, the current study confirms the effectiveness of this relationship in a much shorter time frame, i.e., three months. This study also supports the conclusions of Tierney, Grossman, and Resch (2000), who evaluated the Big Brother/Big Sister Program in the USA. They found that an individual mentoring relationship between a child and an adult enhances the child's self-concept. In addition to the one-to-one relationship, activities with groups of children and mentors (street education, sports, arts, excursion trips, and camping) were vital supports to their growth.

The role of referral organizations (those institutions that provide specialist services and access to a wide variety of opportunities available to children in mainstream society) can not be emphasized enough. A single intervention, such as a one-to-one relationship, is unlikely to bring about major changes or impacts on the life of an at-risk child or youth. They need a series of interventions and positive experiences to continually reinforce their worth, value, and potential for change. The variety of relationships which the program created took into consideration that children respond best to relationships that are not imposed on them. Whether for that reason or others, the variety of relationships greatly contributed to achieving change in the lives of these children.

The study's results indicate that other independent variables had only a limited effect in predicting the overall impact of the Mentoring Program. The child's age had an effect on both the problem solving and vocational maturity variables. This finding is believed to be related to the fact that both sets of variables require the child to use cognitive abilities that enable him/her to find alternatives, assess situations, and make appropriate decisions. Statistically significant differences in cognitive and mental variables were found between the mean of 12th graders' performances and those of 11th graders on the problem-solving scale. Differences favored the older children.

Length of incarceration periods had a significant effect only on vocational maturity. One explanation for this is that children who are more antisocial in their orientation and behavior or who learn to become more antisocial due to the experience of incarceration are usually the ones who are serving longer sentences. These children also have less interest in developing vocational skills and almost categorically have negative views about their futures. This finding was also reflected in gains in scores for self-concept. Children in care facilities (i.e., abandoned but not incarcerated for antisocial acts) had higher scores, those detained for sentencing had lower scores, and the lowest scores were observed in those serving court-mandated sentences.

These findings support the conclusion that the Mentoring Program assists children in adopting a positive self-concept, decreases the level of their social alienation, improves their problem-solving skills, and increases their vocational maturity. Such results contribute to re-integrating these children into society and in helping them avoid repeating behaviors that are associated with risk or violations. Foster (2001) stressed that programs which depend on building relationships between children and adults contribute considerably to lowering crime rates by assisting at-risk children in forming a new life. These early Questscope study results strongly support Foster's emphasis.

It is remarkable that significant changes in children can be fostered in such a short period of time, i.e., after the completion of a minimum of three monthly plans. Factors that made change possible included the multiple supportive relationships that were created around each child (pro-social communities) and the upward mobility that rewarded the full participation of each child (development of competency). This robust effect supports that prosocial mentoring offers a powerful, effective and efficient model for using their society's limited resources to make an unlimited difference in possibilities for such children and their families.

7.5. The Broader Prosocial Community: Prosocially Oriented Programs and Institutions

Questscope, like any voluntary, non-governmental, socially-oriented organization, could function as a self-contained entrepreneurial program competing for resources and dominance in its chosen area of activity. However, doing so would not be consistent with its commitment to a prosocial community model. Rather, Questscope chose to approach other relevant individuals and groups, formal and informal, in a way consistent with a PRSC approach. It also proceeded, despite exceedingly difficult circumstances, to develop itself as a prosocial community. The belief within Questscope has been that this is the only way it can fulfill its commitment to enhance the prosocial aspects of its community and society. Questscope has achieved substantial success in a number of ways.

At the specific program level, Questscope's Mentoring Programs have been established and are functioning in five of the Juvenile Correctional System Centers throughout Jordan. These sites have progressed to the point that Questscope staff no longer work directly on site. A recently implemented street education program has begun at a juvenile detention center for girls. There are currently ten Non-Formal Education Programs throughout Jordan, one of which is for women. In the south of Jordan, Questscope has recently begun an informal street education program for mothers at a women's center. Questscope currently has Volunteer Clubs in universities in four cities in Jordan. In cooperation with the Amman Municipality, Questscope will soon implement additional street education programs in four areas of Amman.

Questscope's Partnership arrangements incorporate a commitment by each partner organization to continue beyond its five years of training and collaboration by becoming part of an overarching group. That group provides ongoing oversight of new Partners' programs as they are begun. Reciprocally, the new member then participates by beginning to assist in overseeing other Partners' programs and expanding the prosocial community approach to other areas in its milieu.

Questscope is leading an effort to form a prosocial community of like-minded organizations, institutions, programs, and community leaders active in Jordan. One manifestation of that initiative was its 2002 Dead Sea Conference whose participants, as mentioned earlier, were directors and/or representatives of major community service agencies and programs throughout Jordan. The agenda included the participants sharing accounts of their projects and plans. Those exchanges highlighted their common emphases on prevention and rehabilitation approaches and highlighted their collective, growing interest and involvement in turning to collaborative and other prosocial community oriented approaches.

Questscope's agenda also includes the creation of a community of policy leaders with a commitment to making constructive prosocial changes in Jordan. The initial meeting led to a tentative agreement among the participants to proceed with the formation of such a community. The one exception was the UNICEF regional director who said his agency is turning away from supporting this and other such pioneering pilot efforts to focus only on funding large-scale projects.

Unfortunately, despite their demonstrated worth, until and unless such agencies can be persuaded of the value of building on empirically grounded and community based approaches like Questscope and the earlier described Residential Youth Program, the growth of such programs faces very substantial obstacles.

Questscope is an organization that seeks to impart its demonstrated ability to other disadvantaged communities for the benefit of all in society. Its goals include: (1) innovation in fields that are currently not responsive to new paradigms for enacting change; (2) innovation in creating roles for action where roles were not envisioned before; (3) assisting people and communities to get some of what they want (key to sustainability); and (4) introducing and applying the three main components of prosocial communities. Establishing this paradigm as the default type of social structure instead of allowing antisocial communities to serve that function would have a profound constructive prosocial effect in communities and, even more broadly, in societies.

This chapter has provided an illustration of an ongoing, comprehensive prosocial community program being successfully implemented and developed. It gives evidence of interrelated accomplishments at the crucial three levels of locality development, social planning, and social action. Further, it shows how these activities have been incorporated as an intrinsic part of Questscope's prosocial community orientation and mode of functioning. It has demonstrated the efficacy of initiating its programs by listening to all of the people involved and cooperating with them at an on-site level to address the problems of their marginalized segments of society. It has combined cooperation and involvement with support of individuals and their formal and informal groups, and interweaving government and non-government funds. The ongoing evolution of these activities and relationships is the crux of prosocial communities, and it needs to be nourished. These bottom-up relationships between individuals and groups are crucial to overcoming the limits of a detached, top-down approach in which experts dismiss grassroots approaches in favor of diagnosing and prescribing solutions from afar, ideologically if not geographically. For example, because they listened to the residents of two neighborhoods in Amman, Questscope's staff was able to learn how different those neighborhoods were and then respond to their specific concerns. Abstract theory and top-down diagnosis could not have identified that information. It was also by direct involvement that Questscope was able to identify the crucial importance of the personal, holistic nature of the Mentoring activities to the overall success of the interlocked facets of locality development, social planning, and social action.

Questscope's development illustrates that the vitality of communities and societies requires the continuing renewal and support of existing programs and the continuing evolution of larger, prosocial community endeavors. When we accept a "we can stop here" mentality, it means that we will continue to consign our projects and programs to their eventual demise. There will always be competing priorities in any community and programs will stagnate without the continuing renewal that those such as Questscope require. We are all faced with deciding whether we want the kinds of benefits that come from a prosocial community orientation.

Finally, Questscope provides a model of how to address particular problem areas or segments of the population by relating them to the overall well-being of the community and society. Its approach emphasizes the benefits, possibly the necessity, of placing the organization's efforts in a prosocial community context. Its results underscore the importance of interrelating formal and non-formal projects and programs as well as governmental and non-governmental organizations in such endeavors. They have shown that informal and formal bureaucratic structures can cooperate in ways that are productive, efficient, and consistent with the integrity of their respective organizations and surpass those which work in isolation. Overall, the broad comprehensive nature of Questscope's outcomes provides a solid basis for encouraging other agencies, institutions, and groups to consider adopting this approach to improve everyone's lives and their communities, not just marginalized groups. That is, by building on the conception of *prosocial communities* as part of a nested framework, including the interrelated concepts of *prosocial competence* and *transcultural ethnic validity*, we have an empirically grounded approach for improving the quality of people's lives across a wide range of cultural circumstances.

Biographical Sketch of Curtis N. Rhodes, Jr. PhD

Curtis N. Rhodes, Jr., PhD was born and raised near Charlotte, NC. He completed a BS in Microbiology and Public Health at Michigan State University (1971), an MPH in Parasitology at the University of North Carolina at Chapel Hill (1976), an MS (1978) and PhD (1980) degrees in the Department of Veterinary Science, University of Wisconsin at Madison (1980). He has resided in the Middle East (Lebanon, Syria, Egypt, Cyprus and Jordan) since 1981. He served as Assistant Dean in the School of Public Health at the American University of Beirut (1981–84); and directed the Near East Foundation in Amman, Jordan (1990–95). Dr. Rhodes founded Questscope (an international non-governmental organization for social development) in 1988 and has been President/International Director of Questscope, based in Amman, Jordan since that date. He has conducted programs in the Middle East for disadvantaged women and youth for almost twenty years; funded by the World Bank, the European Union, USAID, UNICEF, UNODC, various governmental agencies (Canadian, Dutch, Swedish, Japanese and Jordanian), and individual and corporate donors in the UK and USA.

He is a member of the Scientific and Technical Committee for the Child Protection Initiative for the Middle East and North Africa of the Arab Urban Development Institute (AUDI) in Riyadh, Saudi Arabia and sits as an advisor to HM Queen Rania Al Abdullah on the Scientific and Technical Advisory Committee of the National Council for Family Affairs. He is adjunct practice advisor to the Search Institute (Minneapolis, MN) in a Templeton Grant for Child and Adolescent Spiritual Development. He is a Trustee of the Consortium for Street Children, London, England and is also a consultant to the World Bank and the Government of Jordan for issues of disadvantaged children.

Dr. Rhodes is the author or coauthor of various publications and articles related to impact assessment of individual competence and social integration of disadvantaged Arab children (in English); holistic program design for mainstreaming disadvantaged children (also in English); and a five-volume set of manuals for Mentoring "At Risk" Children in Jordan (in Arabic with English translation). He is a contributor to the Jacobs Foundation Series on Adolescence in *Youth and Cities: A Cross-National Perspective.*

Dr Rhodes is a member of the International Society for the Prevention of Child Abuse and Neglect (ISPCAN), the American Scientific Affiliation and mentioned in *Who's Who of Professionals* in 1997.

References

Al-Khouli, T., Al-Zou'bi, H., Mihyar, H., & Rhodes, C. (2006). *Assessment of impact of mentoring on improving the capacities of disadvantaged children to be reintegrated into society* (Submitted for Publication Manuscript).

Al-Kilani, A. & Abbas, H. (1980). *Differences in Self-Concept Scale among orphans and non-orphans of a sample of Jordanian children.* Unpublished manuscript, University of Jordan, Amman, Jordan.

American Psychological Association. (1973). Bylaws, as amended through September 19, 1972. In J. A. Lazo (Ed.), *Biographical directory of the American Psychological Association* (pp. xi–xviii). Washington, DC: Publisher.

Bazerman, M. (2002). Bringing research on judgment, decision making to public policy. *American Psychological Society Bulletin, v. 15(10),* p. 5.

Benjamin, L. B., Jr., & Crouse, E. M. (2002). The American Psychological Association's response to *Brown v. Board of Education. American Psychologist, 57,* 38–50.

Bennett, C. C., Anderson, L. S., Cooper, S., Hassol, L., Klein, D. C., & G. Rosenblum (Eds.), (1966). *Community psychology: A report of the Boston Conference on the education of psychologists for community mental health.* Boston: Boston University Press.

Berger, R. J. & Berger, C. E. (1985). Community organization approaches to the prevention of juvenile delinquency. *Journal of Sociology and Social Welfare, 12,* 129–153.

Berkowitz, B. (1999). Community and neighborhood organization. In J. Rappaport & E. Seidman (Eds.), *Handbook of community psychology* (pp. 764–767). New York: Kluwer Academic/Plenum.

Bishop, B. J. & Syme, G. J. (1992). Social change in rural settings: Lessons for community change agents. In D. R. Thomas & A. Veno. (Eds.), *Psychology and social change* (pp. 93–112). Palmerston North, NZ: The Dunmore Press.

Bond, M. (1999). Gender, race, and class in organizational contexts. *American Journal of Community Psychology, 27,* 327–355.

Boring, E. G. (1929). *A history of experimental psychology.* New York: Appleton-Century.

Chambers, R. (1993). *Challenging the professions: Frontiers for rural development* (pp. 98–102). London: Intermediate Technology Publications.

Chavis, D. M. (1999). Community development and the community psychologist. In J. Rappaport & E. Seidman (Eds.), *Handbook of community psychology* (pp. 767–771). New York: Kluwer Academic/Plenum.

Cherniss, C. & Deegan, G. (1999). The creation of alternative settings. In J. Rappaport & E. Seidman (Eds.), *Handbook of community psychology* (pp. 359–377). New York: Kluwer Academic/Plenum.

Christopher, J. C., Nelson, T., & Nelson, M. D. (2003). Culture and character education: Problems of interpretation in a multicultural society. *Journal of Theoretical and Philosophical Psychology, 23*, 81–101.
Clark, K. B. (1955). *Prejudice and your child.* Boston: Beacon Press.
Clark, K. B. (1965). *Dark ghetto: Dilemmas of social power.* New York: Harper Torchbooks.
Clark, K. B., Chein, I., & Cook, S. W. (2004). The effects of segregation and the consequences of desegregation: A (September 1952) social science statement in the Brown v. Board of Education of Topeka Supreme Court case. *American Psychologist, 59,* 495–501.
Clinton, B. & Larner, M. (1988). Rural community women as leaders in health outreach. *Journal of Primary Prevention, 9,* 13,14.
Cowen, E. (1999). Community psychology and routes to psychological wellness. In J. Rappaport & E. Seidman (Eds.), *Handbook of community psychology* (pp. 79–100). New York: Kluwer Academic/Plenum.
Crites, J. O. & Savickas, M. L. (1995). *Career Maturity Inventory sourcebook*, Toronto, Canada: Careerware.
D'Augelli, A. (1990). Community development and the HIV epidemic: The development of helping communities. *The Journal of Community Psychology, 18,* 337–346.
Dean, D. G. (1961). Alienation: Its meaning and measurement. *American Sociological Review, 26*, 53–758.
Deci, E. L. (1975). *Intrinsic motivation.* New York: Plenum.
D'Ercole, A. & Streuning, E. (1990). Victimization among homeless women: Implications for service delivery. *Journal of Community Psychology, 18,* 141–152.
Ennew, J. (2002, October, 24–27). Children's participation: Experience and reflections. Keynote address at International Workshop on Child Participation Action. Beijing, China.
Felner, R. D., Felner, T. Y., & Silverman, M. M. (1999). Prevention in mental health and social intervention: Conceptual and methodological issues in the evolution of the science and practice of prevention. In J. R. Rappaport & E. Seidman (Eds.), *Handbook of community psychology*, (pp. 9–42). New York: Kluwer Academic/Plenum.
Fine, M. (2004). The power of the Brown v. Board of Education Decision: Theorizing threats to sustainability. *American Psychologist, 59*, 502–510.
Foa, U. G., Converse, J., Jr., Tornblom, K. Y., & Foa, E. B. (1993). *Resource theory: Explorations and applications.* San Diego, CA: Academic Press.
Folkman, S. & Moskowitz, J. T. (2004). Coping: Pitfalls and promise. In S. T. Fiske, D. L. Schacter, & C. Zahn-Waxler (Eds.), *Annual Review of Psychology* (pp. 745–774). Palo Alto, CA: Annual Reviews.
Foster, L. (2001). *Effectiveness of mentor programs: Review of the literature from 1995 to 2000* (California Research Bureau, California, USA. ISBN #: 1–58073–136–1).
Gatz, M., Barbarin, O., Tyler, F. B., Mitchell, R., Morgan, J., Wirzbicki, P., Crawford, J., & Engleman, A. (1982). Enhancement of individual and community competence: The older adult as community worker. *American Journal of Community Psychology, 10,* 291–303.
Giddens, A. (1990). *The Consequences of modernity.* Stanford, CA: Stanford University Press.
Goldenberg, I. I. (1971). *Build me a mountain: Youth, poverty, and the creation of new settings.* Cambridge, MS: The MIT Press.

Grossman, J. B. & Rhodes, J. E. (2002). The test of time: Predictors and effects of duration in youth mentoring relationships. *American Journal of Community Psychology, 30,* 199–219.

Guttman, D. (1977). The cross-cultural perspective: Notes toward a comparative psychology of aging. In J. E. Birren & K. M. Schaie (Eds.), *Handbook of the psychology of aging* (pp. 302–336). New York: Van Nostrand Reinhold.

Haggbloom, S. J., Warnick, R., Warnick, J. E., Jones, V. K., Yarbrough, G. L., Russell, T. M., Borecky, C. M., McGahhey, R., Powell, J. L., Beavers, J., & Monte, E. (2002). The 100 most eminent psychologists of the 20th century. *Review of General Psychology, 6(2),* 139–152.

Hardister, R. (1985, July). *Establishing and maintaining relationships in local development practice.* [Local Community Development Services, Egypt] Cairo, Egypt: Near East Foundation Publishing, 1990. n. p.

Heller, K., Jenkins, R. A., Steffen, A. M., & Swindle R. W. Jr., (1999).In J. Rappaport & E. Seidman (Eds.), *Handbook of community psychology* (pp. 445–470). New York: Kluwer Academic/Plenum.

Heppner, P. P. & Peterson, C. H. (1982). The development and implications of a Personal Problem-Solving Inventory. *Journal of Counseling Psychology, 29,* 66–75.

Hersch, C. (1972). Social history, mental health, and community control. *American Psychologist, 27(8),* 749–754.

Hua, S. (2005). A perfect world. *Wilson Quarterly, XXIX, 4,* 62–67.

Hunter, A., & Riger, S. (1986). The meaning of community in community mental health. *Journal of Community Psychology, 14,* 5–71.

Jahoda, M. (1950). Toward a social psychology of mental health. In M. J. E. Senn (Ed.), *Symposium on the healthy personality.* New York: Josiah Macy, Jr. Foundation.

Jahoda, M. (1958). *Current concepts of positive mental health.* New York: Basic Books.

Kagitcibasi, C. (1996). *Family and human development across cultures: A view from the other side.* Mahwah, NJ: Lawrence Erlbaum Associates.

Katz, R. (1984). Empowerment and synergy: Expanding the community's healing resources. *Prevention in Human Services, 3,* 201–226.

Katz, R. & Seth, N. (1987). Synergy and healing: A perspective on Western health care. *Prevention in human services, 5,* 109–136.

Kelly, J. G., Ryan, A. M., Altman, B. E., & Stelzner, S. P. (1999). Understanding and changing social systems: An ecological view. In J. Rappaport & E. Seidman (Eds.), *Handbook of community psychology* (pp 133–159). New York: Kluwer Academic/Plenum.

Keppel, B. (2002). Kenneth B. Clark in the patterns of American culture. *American Psychologist, 57,* 29–37.

Kochanska, G. (2002). Mutually responsive orientation between mothers and their young children: A context for the early development of conscience. *Current Directions in Psychological Science, 11,* 191–195.

Kohlberg, L. (1969). *Stages in the development of moral thought and action.* New York: Holt, Rinehart & Winston.

Kotter, J. P. & Haskett, J. L. (1992). *Corporate culture and performance.* New York: Free Press.

Krebs, D. L. & Denton, K. (2005). A pragmatic approach to morality: A critical evaluation of Kohlberg's model. *Psychological Review, 112,* 629–649.

Lave, J. & Wenger, E. (1991). *Situated learning: Legitimate peripheral participation.* Cambridge University Press: Cambridge.

Lefcourt, H. M. (Ed.). (1984). *Research with the locus of control construct* (Vol. 3). New York: Academic Press.
Maton, K. I. & Hrabowski III, F. A. (2004). Increasing the number of African American PhDs in the sciences and engineering: A strengths-based approach. *American Psychologist, 59*, 547–556.
McCormick, R. M. (1997). Healing through interdependence: The role of connecting in First Nations healing practices. *Canadian Journal of Counselling, 31(3)*, 172–184.
Molden, D. C. & Dweck, C. S. (2006). Finding "meaning" in psychology. *American Psychologist, 61*, 192–203.
Morgan, J. R. (1999). Applied community psychology: A ten-year field trial. In J. Rappaport & E. Seidman (Eds.), *Handbook of community psychology* (pp. 745–748). New York: Kluwer Academic/Plenum.
Nelson, G., Prilleltensky, I. & MacGillivary, H. (2001). Building value-based partnerships: Toward solidarity with oppressed groups. *American Journal of Community Psychology, 29*, 649–677.
No Child Left Behind Act of 2001, Pub. L. No. 107–110, 115 Stat. 1425 (2002).
Olweus, D. (1991). Bully/victim problems among schoolchildren: Basic facts and effects of a school-based intervention program. In D. J. Pepler & K. H. Rubin (Eds.), *Development and treatment of childhood aggression* (pp. 411–448). Hillsdale, NJ: Erlbaum.
Olweus, D. (1992). Victimization among school children: Intervention and prevention. In G. W. Albee, L. A. Bond, & T. V. C. Monsey (Eds.), *Improving children's lives: Global perspectives on prevention* (pp. 279–295). Newbury Park: Sage.
Olweus, D. (2003). A profile of bullying at school. *Educational Leadership, 60*, 12–17.
Peck, M. S. (1988). *The different drum: Community making and peace.* New York: Simon and Schuster.
Pickren, W. P. & Tomes, H. (2002). The legacy of Kenneth B. Clark to the APA: The Board of Social and Ethical Responsibility for Psychology. *American Psychologist, 57*, 51–59.
Quarrey, M., & Rosen, C. (1994). *Employee ownership and corporate performance.* Oakland, CA: National Center for Employee Ownership.
Questscope. Retrieved March 5, 2006, from http://www.questscope.org/aboutus.htm.
Random House Webster's collegiate dictionary (2nd Ed). (1999). New York: Random House, Inc.
Rappaport, J. R. (1981). In praise of paradox: A social policy of empowerment over prevention. *American Journal of Community Psychology, 9*, 1–25.
Rappaport, J. R., & Seidman, E. (Eds.), (1999). *Handbook of community psychology*. New York: Kluwer Academic/Plenum.
Rawls, J. (1971). *A theory of justice.* Cambridge: Harvard University Press.
Reinharz, S. (1984). Alternative settings and social change. In K. Heller, R. H. Price, S. Reinharz, S. Riger, & A. Wandersman (Eds.), *Psychology and community change* (2nd ed., pp. 286–336). Homewood, IL: Dorsey Press.
Rhodes, C. N., (1998). *Children out of place.* Unpublished paper, Questscope: Amman, Jordan.
Rhodes, C. N., Mihyar, H.A., Al-Bustami, G. J., & Al-Khouli, T. (2004, January 7–9). *Assessing mentoring as an approach to restoring youth competence: A prospective study of impact and life changes in disadvantaged Arab/Jordanian children.* Presented at Children and Mediterranean Conference, Genoa, Italy.

Rigby, K., & Bagshaw, D. (2003). Prospects of adolescent students collaborating with teachers in addressing isues of bullying and conflict in schools. *Educational Psychology, 23,* 535–546.

Rogers, E. M. (1995). *Diffusion of innovations* (6th ed.). New York: Free Press.

Ryan, M. (1997, March 2). I realized that change had to start with me. *Parade Magazine.* p. 1.

Sameroff, A. J., & Fiese, B. H. (1989). Conceptual issues in prevention. In D. Schaffer, I. Phillips, N. B. Enzer, M. M. Silverman, & V. Anthony (Eds.), *Prevention of mental disorders alcohol and other drug use in children and adolescents: OSAP prevention monograph-2* (pp. 23–45). Washington, D.C.: U. S. Government Printing Office.

Sarason, S. B. (1972). *The creation of settings and the future societies.* San Francisco: Jossey-Bass.

Sarason, S. B. & Lorentz, E. (1979). *The challenge of the resource exchange network.* San Francisco, CA.: Jossey-Bass.

Segall, M. H., Dasen, P. R., Berry, J. W., & Poortinga, Y. H. (1999). *Human behavior in global perspective: An introduction to cross-cultural psychology (2nd ed.).* Boston: Allyn & Bacon.

Selbourne, D. (2001). *The principle of duty.* Notre Dame, IN: University of Notre Dame Press.

Shinn, M., & Perkins, D. N. T. (1999). Contributions from organizational psychology. In Rappaport, J, R, & Seidman, E. (Eds.), *Handbook of community psychology* (pp. 615–645). New York: Kluwer Academic/Plenum.

Singer, P. (2002). *The ethics of globalization.* New Haven: Yale University Press.

Smith, M. B. (1950). Optima of mental health. *Psychiatry, 13,* 503–510.

Snowden, L. R., Martinez, M., & Morris, A. (1999). Community psychology and ethnic minority populations. In J. Rappaport & E. Seidman (Eds.), *Handbook of community psychology* (pp. 833–855). New York: Kluwer Academic/Plenum.

Stark, W. (1992). Empowerment and social change: Health promotion within the healthy cities project of WHO–Steps toward a participative prevention program. In Albee, G. W., Bond, L. A., & Monsey, T. V. C. (Eds.), *Improving children's lives: Global perspectives on prevention* (pp. 167–176). Newbury Park: Sage.

Swift, C., Bond, M. A., & Serrano-Garcia, I. (1999). Women's empowerment: A review of community psychology's first twenty-five years. In J. Rappaport & E. Seidman (Eds.), *Handbook of community psychology* (pp. 857–895). New York: Kluwer Academic/Plenum.

Swift, C. & Levin, G. (1987). Empowerment: An emerging mental health technology. *Journal of primary prevention, 7,* 242–263.

Tierney, J. P., Grossman, J. B. & Resch, N. L. (2000). *Making a difference: An impact study of Big Brothers Big Sisters.* Public/Private Ventures: Philadelphia, PA.

Trickett, E. J., Barone, C., & Watts, R. (1999) Contextual influences in mental health consultation. In J. Rappaport & E. Seidman (Eds.), *Handbook of community psychology* (pp. 303–330). New York: Kluwer Academic/Plenum.

Tyler, F. B. (1973). Adolescent competence: A different point of view. *Virginia Medical Monthly, 100,* 919–926.

Tyler, F. B. (June, 1997). *Urban settings, youth violence, and prosocial communities.* Paper presented at Urban Childhood Conference, Trondheim, Norway.

Tyler, F. B. (2001). *Cultures, communities, competence, and change.* New York: Kluwer/Plenum.

Tyler, F. B., Brome, D. R., & Williams, J. E. (1991). *Ethnic validity, ecology, and psychotherapy.* New York: Plenum.

Tyler, F. B., Dhawan, N., & Sinha, Y. (1988). Adaptation patterns of Indian and American adolescents. *Journal of Social Psychology, 128,* 633–645.

Tyler, F. B., Pargament, K. I., & Gatz, M. (1983). The resource collaborator role: A model for interaction between change agents and community members. *American Psychologist, 38,* 388–398.

Tyler, F. B., Tyler, S. L., Echeverry, J., & Zea, M. (1991). Making it on the streets in Bogota; A psychosocial study of street youth. *Genetic, social, and general psychology monographs, 117,* 395–417.

Tyler, L. (1969). APA in public affairs: Report of the ad hoc Committee on Public Affairs. *American Psychologist, 24,* 1–4.

Tyler, S. L., Tyler, F. B., Dhawan, N., Punetha, D., & Sinha, Y. (August, 1996). Family conflict/violence in India. Paper read at the XIII Congress of the International Congress of Cross-Cultural Psychology, Montreal, Canada.

Tyler, T. R., Boeckman, R. J., Smith, H. J., & Huo, Y. J. (1997). *Social justice in a diverse society.* Boulder, CO: Westview Press.

van Uchelen, C. (1999). Individualism, collectivism, and community psychology. In J. Rappaport & E. Seidman (Eds.), *Handbook of community psychology* (pp. 65–78). New York: Kluwer Academic/Plenum.

van Uchelen, C., Davidson, S. F., Quressette, S., Brasfield, C., & Demerais, L. (1997). What makes us strong: Urban aboriginal perspectives on wellness and strength. *Canadian Journal of Mental Health, 16(2),* 37–50.

Veno, A. & Veno, E. (1992). Managing public order at the Australian Motorcycle Grand Prix. In D. R. Thomas & A. Veno. (Eds.), *Psychology and social change* (pp. 74–92). Palmerston North, NZ: The Dunmore Press.

Volpi, E. (2002). *Street Children: Promising practices and approaches.* Washington, DC.: The World Bank Institute.

Weinstein, R. S. (2002). Overcoming inequality in schooling: A call to action for community psychology. *American Journal of Community Psychology, 30,* 21–42.

Weinstein, R. S., Gregory, A., & Strambler, M. J. (2004). Intractable self-fulfilling prophecies: Fifty years after Brown v. Board of Education. *American Psychologist, 59,* 511–520.

Werner, E. E. (1989). High risk in young adulthood: A longitudinal study from birth to 32 years. *American Journal of Orthopsychiatry, 59(1),* 72–81.

Wolff, T. (1999). Practitioners' perspectives. In J. Rappaport & E. Seidman (Eds.), *Handbook of community psychology* (pp. 741–745). New York: Kluwer Academic/Plenum.

Zimmerman, M. A. (1999). Empowerment theory: Psychological, organizational, and community levels of analysis. In J. Rappaport & E. Seidman (Eds.), *Handbook of community psychology* (pp. 43–63). New York: Kluwer Academic/Plenum.

Subject Index

Author Index

GPSR Compliance

The European Union's (EU) General Product Safety Regulation (GPSR) is a set of rules that requires consumer products to be safe and our obligations to ensure this.

If you have any concerns about our products, you can contact us on ProductSafety@springernature.com

In case Publisher is established outside the EU, the EU authorized representative is:

Springer Nature Customer Service Center GmbH
Europaplatz 3
69115 Heidelberg, Germany

Batch number: 10844692

Printed by Printforce, the Netherlands